First Fridays with the Sacred Heart

by the Rev. L. Nauer, M.S.C.

Permissu Superiorum: Joseph J. Janssen, M.S.C.
Provencial

NIHIL OBSTAT: Chas. R. Kelly, *Censor Librorum*
January 9, 1944

IMPRIMATUR: John J. Boylan, D.D., *Bishop of Rockford*
January 7, 1944

NATAL PUBLISHING LLC
ARS LONGA, VITA BREVIS

Cover art by Mauricio A. from Pixabay

CONTENTS

Litany of the Most Holy Name of Jesus
Litany of the Blessed Virgin Mary
Litany in Honor of Saint Joseph

Preface

This little volume which I herewith place in your hands, dear readers, wishes to speak to your heart, not only within church walls, but also in the solitude of your own home.

The object of its coming is twofold: as a little messenger of the Sacred Heart, it shall introduce you to the beautiful devotion to the Sacred Heart, and shall induce you to gather fruits of sanctity from its practice.

Notwithstanding its exceedingly wide dissemination, this devotion is for many, alas, a book "sealed with seven seals." Frequently it is still looked down upon as a product of exaggerated piety.

This book wishes to show you how erroneous such a conception is. For the devotion to the Sacred Heart has been given to our own age by God Himself, in order to restore the entire world in Christ, and to imbue it with the ardent zeal of the early Christians. Fundamentally, this devotion is nothing new in the Church. Only its external part, the shell, is new; the internal part, its soul, is as old as Christianity. You will understand this better if you will read attentively the first part of this book, which in an easily understood way sets forth the origin and propagation, the object and purpose, and finally the practice of the devotion to the Sacred Heart.

The devotion to the Sacred Heart has been approved and promoted by the Church, not because it was revealed to Saint Margaret Mary, but because it agrees perfectly with Christian Revelation, with the Gospel and with the Fathers of the Church. In order to make that clear to you, I have inserted in the second part of this book, for each First Friday, a text drawn from the Gospels, and have added a short meditation upon each. These meditations form the spiritual framework of the little volume. From them arise, quite spontaneously, the twelve Devotions for Holy Communion, which are designed to assist you in the practical application of the Devotion to the Sacred Heart.

The Apostles and disciples of Christ, as also the early Christians, who knew the God-Man in person, considered it a matter of course that a Christian, present daily at the Holy Sacrifice, should also receive the Body of the Lord daily. That was practical devotion to the Sacred Heart in the best sense of the word. Can it be, then, that the monthly Communion on the First Friday (or Sunday) should be mistaken for exaggerated piety?

May this little book promote devotion and love toward the Heart of the Savior; and may it further the devout observance of the First Fridays, which is so rich in blessings.

THE AUTHOR

Part I: A Short Treatise on Devotion to the Sacred Heart

ORIGIN AND HISTORY OF THE DEVOTION TO THE SACRED HEART

1. ***Revelations Made by Jesus to St. Margaret Mary Alacoque***
    On June 20, 1671, the saintly virgin, Margaret Mary Alacoque, entered the convent of the Visitation at Paray le Monial in France. It was soon recognized that this humble nun was especially favored by God and called to an extraordinary vocation. On the very day of her profession the first signs of her future sanctity were made manifest. She relates: "On that day He blessed me with His divine presence in a manner which I had never experienced previously. I saw my divine Spouse, felt Him near me, and heard His voice, much better than if I had experienced all this through my bodily senses."

    From now on the ecstasies occurred frequently, and the revelations were more distinct, especially on the First Friday of each month. We shall give particular consideration to three of these revelations.

    The first occurred most probably on December 27, 1673. Wrapt in deep devotion, Margaret Mary was kneeling before the Blessed Sacrament, when she felt herself so completely surrounded by the presence of God that time and place were entirely forgotten. She tells us: "My Lord permitted me to repose on His breast for some time; and He revealed to me the wonders of His love as well as the indescribable mysteries of His Sacred Heart, which until then had been hidden from me." Now, for the first time, He also revealed to her His Heart as we see It pictured, and said to her: "My Heart is so replete with love for men, and especially for you, that the flames of Its love can no longer be restrained. Through your mediation My Heart must pour Itself out for men to enrich them with Its treasures. As to the value of these treasures, know that they contain graces for salvation through which alone mankind can be saved from the abyss of destruction. I have chosen you for the accomplishment of My purpose despite your unworthiness and lack of knowledge, in order that all this may be more easily recognized as My work."

The second important revelation took place in the year 1674. Again Margaret Mary knelt before the Blessed Sacrament, absorbed in earnest prayer, when Jesus, radiant in divine glory, appeared to her. His five wounds shone like five suns, His sacred breast resembled a burning furnace, and the light and fire seemed to stream from His Heart as if from a living and inexhaustible fountain.

Our Lord complained bitterly of man's ingratitude, adding that this was the cause of His greatest suffering during the Passion. "If men were more grateful, all that I have done for them would be trifling in My eyes. But they remain unmoved and repay all My love with contempt. Grant me the comfort that you, at least, strive to make reparation for this ingratitude." Hereupon our Lord commanded her to receive Holy Communion as often as permitted, but especially on the First Friday of each month; furthermore, He bade her to watch with Him and pray for sinners on every Thursday evening from eleven to twelve o'clock.

Finally, during the Octave of Corpus Christi in the year 1675, Margaret Mary received the most important revelation regarding the Sacred Heart. Jesus appeared to her and said: "You cannot give Me greater proof of your love than by doing all that I have so often requested of you." Then He opened His Heart with these words: "Behold this Heart Which has so loved men as to spare nothing, even exhausting and consuming Itself in proof of Its love. As a recompense I receive from most men only ingratitude, through the contempt, irreverence, sacrileges and lukewarmness toward this Sacrament of Love. But what grieves me most deeply is that even hearts consecrated to Me treat Me thus. I therefore request of you that the First Friday after the Octave of Corpus Christi be designated as a special feast in honor of My Heart. On this day a solemn act of reparation shall be made and Holy Communion received worthily, in order to atone for the insults to which My Heart was exposed during the exposition on the altar during the Octave. I promise you that My Heart shall expand, to pour out abundantly the blessings of Its love upon all who thus honor It and cause others to do so."

Margaret Mary felt herself in nowise capable of fulfilling this mandate. "Alas, O Lord," she said, "to whom are You come? To a great sinner, who in her unworthiness would be much more likely to frustrate the fulfillment of Your purpose." But the Lord did not desist: "Do you not know that I make use of the weak in order to confound the mighty, and that I manifest My power especially to the humble and poor in spirit? Therefore, call upon my servant, Father Claude de la Colombiere, and in My Name tell him to make every effort to introduce this devotion and thus bring joy to My Heart. Bid him not to permit himself to become discouraged by the difficulties with which he will have to contend, but to remember that whoever distrusts himself and places his full confidence in God will certainly succeed."

The humble and devout Jesuit at once declared himself ready to be a willing instrument in the hand of the Lord. In the pulpit and the confessional, in monasteries as well as among the laity, by word of mouth and in his writings, he labored constantly to propagate the devotion to the Sacred Heart among all "that looked for the redemption of Israel."

Margaret Mary would rather have remained silent regarding her visions on account of the opposition of some nuns and because her humility led her to believe that she, a great sinner, could not be a handmaid of the Lord. But He who had selected her as the promulgator of this devotion allowed her no respite. "I require for My Heart a victim which will consume itself entirely for the fulfillment of My desires; you shall be the one. I desire no other victim, therefore have I chosen you."

Then He foretold that the very Sisters of her community, who now were the most vehement in their opposition, would later cooperate with the greatest zeal. And this came to pass. In a short time there occurred a complete change of views. The devotion was now practiced by all the Sisters, and soon there was noticed a gratifying progress in their spiritual life. The other convents of the Visitation nuns also took up this devotion with evident success.

Margaret Mary was highly pleased and wrote thus to a monk: "I know of no other devotion in the spiritual life more fitted to lead a soul to the highest perfection in a short time. Endeavor to induce all religious to practice this devotion, for it will cause such a great stimulus in their spiritual life that no other means shall be necessary to restore the first zeal in the punctual observance of religious life and to lead the saintly to still greater perfection in following the holy rules."

2.   The Spread of the Devotion to the Sacred Heart

This devotion, so favored by blessings, could not remain confined to the seclusion of convents. The Lord had requested of Margaret Mary the institution of a public devotion and feast of expiation. The picture of His Heart, flaming with love, was to be placed in every church and home.

Indeed, the prophecies which Jesus had made to Margaret Mary began to be fulfilled at once. The devotion to the Sacred Heart found an enthusiastic reception among the people. Altars and chapels in honor of the Sacred Heart were erected everywhere, and societies in Its honor were established in all Catholic countries and even in the distant mission fields.

The saintly virgin, Margaret Mary, was not permitted, however, to witness the culmination of her life's work on earth. She died on October 17, 1690, in the odor of sanctity.

At last, in 1856, one hundred and eighty-one years after Christ had made His request to Margaret Mary, Pope Pius IX ordained that the Feast of the Sacred Heart should be observed annually in the entire Church. This was the signal for a great increase in the spread of the devotion, which was further augmented by the fact that on August 19, 1864, Margaret Mary was solemnly declared Blessed. Fifty-six years later, in 1920, she was elevated to sainthood by Pope Benedict XV.

During the afflictions of 1870, the laity as well as the hierarchy recognized more and more the fact that only in the Sacred Heart of Jesus were to be found salvation and security against the principal evils of modern times, namely, the spirit of revolution and the destruction of the entire social order. Five hundred and twenty-five bishops petitioned the Holy Father to dedicate all the churches of the Catholic world to the Sacred Heart. Soon thereafter on June 16, 1875, Pius IX sent to all bishops a form of Consecration which was to be recited in all the Catholic churches of the world.

On June 28, 1889, Pope Leo XIII raised the Feast of the Sacred Heart to the dignity of a first-class feast for the whole Church. On May 11, 1899, he decreed the consecration of the world to the Sacred Heart and sent the Act of Consecration to all bishops. Pope Pius XI, in his encyclical on the Sacred Heart, suggested a union of prayer and reparation in preparation for the Feast of the Sacred Heart. "The proper spirit of this solemnity is the spirit of loving reparation, and, therefore, on that day every year in perpetuity there should be made in all the churches of the world a public act of reparation for all the offenses that wound that Divine Heart."

3. ***The Heart of Jesus, Object of the Devotion to the Sacred Heart***

My dear reader, enter with me into the sanctuary of the Sacred Heart of Jesus. I invite you in the words of the Prophet Isaias: "Come, let us go up to the mountain of the Lord, and to the house of the God of Jacob, and He will teach us His ways, and we will walk in His paths" (Is. 2:3). Yes, let us ascend to the citadel of divine love, to the Heart of our God.

But before we enter, permit me to ask a somewhat worldly question: Have you ever felt a very tender and strong love toward a fellow being? Certainly, because you are human, and nothing human is alien to you. Is it not true that you felt an inner longing for the object of your love? Was not your heart stirred as if it were to leap forth from its bounds and bring to light the love which consumed it? Oh, what a happy and contented feeling filled your heart when your love found response! But when there was no response to your love, no recognition of your affection, you felt heavy at heart and depressed in spirit.

Let us now enter into the Heart of Jesus; there you will see that God has loved us with an infinitely greater measure of love. He Himself has said: "With eternal love have I loved thee. As a mother loveth her only-begotten son, so have I loved thee – and even though a mother should forget her only son, nevertheless I could not forget thee."

Thus spoke God in the Old Testament. But all these protestations of His love found only deaf ears and cold hearts among men. Heaven was too exalted, and they themselves lay too deep in the mire of sin; yes, they feared the One who ruled so far away in the solitude of the heavens. "Can anyone love us who lives so far and high above us in inaccessible light?" Thus they blasphemed His eternal love. Conditions probably would have continued as they were, heaven remaining dark and the earth desolate and dreary, if God had not wrought an inconceivable miracle of His love. Because men did not wish to believe in His eternal love, He determined to love them with a created human heart. And so the miraculous, unprecedented and unbelievable came to pass: the invisible God became man even as you and I: He became one among us. In His breast pulsated a Heart as human as ours, a Heart which loved and desired to be loved even as ours, a Heart which embraced all, yes, all human beings, and which desired but one thing: men's appreciation of Its love! Do you know this Heart? It is the Heart of Jesus, the object of the devotion to the Sacred Heart.

Why should we not be permitted to venerate this Heart? The hearts of deceased kings and of noted men often are kept in precious reliquaries and persevered from corruption. In Altötting, Bavaria, above the miraculous altar of the Mother of God, we find the hearts of the Bavarian kings, placed there as a most precious legacy to the Patroness of that country. Yet, these are but lifeless hearts, dust and ashes, powerless remains of kings who have laid down their scepters in death and have gone the way of all flesh.

But, if that is so, then what of the Heart of the noblest and purest, most humble and meek, most glorious and regal of men? What of the Heart of the God-Man, of the Messianic King, whose sovereignty is bounded by neither space nor time; a Heart not dead, shapeless and preserved in a cold receptacle, but a Heart which beats with eternal youth in the breast of the glorified God-Man? Is it possible that we should not be allowed to venerate It? This Heart has loved men without exception to such a degree that It did not spare but rather consumed Itself (entirely) in order to prove Its love, and even now is so filled with love for us that It cannot repress the flames of that love – can it be that we should not be free to adore that Heart?

Is the heart the seat or organ love? An idle question. As long as I know that love finds its strongest response in the heart, I feel impelled to listen to the beat of that Heart which has the greatest love, the Heart upon which I must depend for the rekindling of my own sad and lovelorn heart. To love this Heart with a transcendent love is a solace which is beyond all human consolation.

I do not know why so many writers on the subject of the devotion to the Sacred Heart pass over so lightly and timidly its consoling side as if they feared to lose sight of the principal object of this devotion, namely, divine love, the symbol of which is the human Heart of Jesus.

But why should we not venerate the humanity of Christ, His human Heart and His human love? Did not the Son of God become man in order to be one of us, like us in everything, except sin? Is it not edifying, touching and instructive in the highest degree to consider the human manner in which the Son of God acts, thinks, feels and speaks – out of the super-abundance of His human Heart? Certainly, one is never allowed to separate the humanity from the divinity of Christ. But that should not prevent us from showing special gratitude to His human Heart. If I understand correctly the revelations made by Christ to St. Margaret Mary, it is just this human love which He wishes recognized and which He desires us to reciprocate.

Christian soul, if you reflect and meditate upon the human love of your Saviour, you will reach a better understanding of His divine love.

Behold, He calls with His sweet voice: "Come to Me, all you that are burdened and heavily laden, and I will refresh you." This was not said in a sudden outburst of His Heart's love, but rather because of His Heart's eternal desire, an infinite, and irresistible longing which caused Him to become man. Our divine Saviour Himself has said: "God so loved the world (that is mankind) that He gave His only-begotten Son." Therefore the entire life of the God-Man, Jesus Christ, is nothing else but the natural consequence and the visible expression of His divine love. Only one thought inspired Him, only one love consumed His Heart: He longed to reveal God's love to men, to enkindle within them the fire of divine love, and thus to lead them to a union of love with God.

Have you ever stood on the beach and permitted your gaze to wander over the endless expanse of the ocean? You could not measure, but only imagine, its length, breadth and depth. You saw a swell of the sea break upon the shore, then another and another, and so on and on . . . Ah, you could have watched for hours this never-ending surf. In just the same way every pulse of the Heart of Jesus and every emotion of His human soul are, as it were, the interminable surf on the ocean of God's eternal love. And this mysterious surge continues forever and ever: here on earth in the Blessed Sacrament of the Altar, and in heaven within the Heart of the Son of God. The inhabitants of the heavenly Jerusalem will hear in blissful ecstasy the heartbeats of the infinite love of God, and will extol and praise the Heart of Jesus as the living emblem of the incomprehensible love of God for man.

For that reason the devotion to the Sacred Heart will never end, but will enjoy its crowning fulfillment in heaven, where the divine love will stream from the Heart of the Son of God in supreme bliss and happiness. Truly, no eye has seen, nor ear heard, neither has it entered into the mind of man what God has prepared for those who love and venerate the Sacred Heart of Jesus.

Dear reader, do you perceive the trend of thought in the preceding chapter? In order that you may comprehend it more fully I shall repeat it briefly. The object of the devotion to the Sacred Heart is the human Heart of Jesus, not lifeless, but a truly living Heart. It is the Heart which is constantly active in the sacred humanity of Christ, active in its emotions, feelings and impulses, especially in Its immense love for us. But this Heart is not merely the heart of a man, but the Heart of the Son of God, inseparably a part of Him in the true sense of the word: the Heart of the God-Man, and therefore worthy of highest reverence, namely, adoration. Moreover, because the Son of God has assumed human nature, and consequently a human heart in order to manifest His infinite love, the Sacred Heart of Jesus is also the living and natural symbol of His divine love. This living Heart of Jesus Christ, therefore, which is so powerfully moved by the human love of Christ, and which is in such intimate relationship with the divine love and symbolic of this love, is the object of the devotion to the Sacred Heart.

You may ask: "Why do we adore this divine-human Heart of Christ and His love . . . why not simply Christ?" We do this because we wish to penetrate more deeply into the mysteries of the sacred Person of Christ; we do this because we wish to recall more fully the benefits bestowed upon us by His love, and therefore, we picture to ourselves the living Heart of Jesus enflamed with love, and choose It as the very object of our veneration, adoration and love.

We human beings have a certain fault. We do not readily believe in the disinterested love of others for us, mainly because our own love is not free from selfishness and egotism. We demand irrefutable proof. That we might have abundant proof of His infinite love, Jesus has exposed His most Sacred Heart, revealed His love for us, and thereby has given us the most powerful expression of His unreserved self-abandonment for our salvation: "Behold the Heart which has loved men so much." . . . "My heart is so full of love for men that It can no longer restrain the flames of that love."

The revelations which Jesus made to St. Margaret Mary remind me of a saying of Christ: "An evil and adulterous generation seeketh a sign: and a sign shall not be given it, but the sign of Jonas the Prophet" (Matt. 12: 39). Sixteen hundred years had passed since these words were spoken. For sixteen hundred years the Church of Christ had fulfilled her divine mission on earth. What an enormous number of favors were granted in those centuries! And yet, the Christian world had become indifferent, cold and ungrateful! The unchristian spirit of selfishness and uncharitableness penetrated into all classes of society, even into the sanctuary, into the ranks of priests and bishops. The time had come when God was to give a new sign of His love. Indeed, the present generation calls for a sign, but it will receive no other sign but that of the Sacred Heart of Jesus, aflame with love, crowned with thorns and surmounted by the cross.

4. *The Aim of the Devotion to the Sacred Heart*

A sorrowful complaint about the ingratitude of men is noticeable in all the revelations which Jesus made to St. Margaret Mary. Day and night He remains in the tabernacles on our altars, because it is His joy to be among the children of men. But alas, only a few seem to care; and even those who are especially dedicated to His service are often lukewarm or cold in His presence. Silence is the answer to the voice of the lonely dweller in the tabernacle while He calls, "All you who pass by this way, behold and see whether there is sorrow like unto My sorrow."

The devotion to the Sacred Heart is intended to end this

cheerless isolation of the Redeemer. Its purpose is to lead men to a greater knowledge of the infinite love of the Saviour, to induce them to return this love, to repair the insults heaped upon Him, and thus to attain a closer union with the Lord.

A. *You will gain a knowledge of Christ and His love through the earnest contemplation of His life and Passion, and particularly through devout meditation on the most Blessed Sacrament of the Altar.* The saints in heaven are so completely wrapt in this love of God that they find their greatest happiness in the beatific vision, because they see Him face to face, know Him as He is. "Now this is eternal life: that they may know Thee, the only true God, and Jesus Christ whom Thou hast sent" (John 17:3). his will be your reward if you often gaze upon the Sacred Heart of Jesus. But you may say: "I have often looked at the image of the Sacred Heart, but it has told me nothing, and I have felt no benefit." Your devotion, my dear reader, must not be so superficial. The picture of the Sacred Heart does not constitute the devotion; it only helps to rouse it within us. If you wish to learn about the Heart of Jesus, you must read the Gospels, Bible history, or some authorized books on the life of Christ, and study the Person of Christ with attention and devotion; how He healed the sick, comforted the sorrowing, and gently led sinners to repentance; how He traveled zealously through all parts of Palestine preaching the Kingdom of God; how earnestly He defended the honor of God and the sanctity of the house of God. Everywhere you will recognize the love of His Sacred Heart.

B. *Christian soul, study and fathom as much as possible the love of your Saviour, because that is the first aim of the devotion to the Sacred Heart; then you will reach also its second aim, namely, responsive love.* St. Margaret Mary designates this as the principal goal of the devotion; she writes: "The Lord shall rule in spite of His enemies, and constitute Himself Lord and Master of our hearts, because His principal aim in this devotion is to lead men to love Him." But do not be deceived. I am not by any means speaking of an emotional piety which arises from and ends in feelings, but of a piety which is based on the sincere and firm will to regulate your life and to put it in perfect harmony with the will of God, to resist the inordinate desires of your own heart and fortify it against the temptations of the world. As proof of a corresponding love from us, the divine Saviour desires of the followers and adorers of His Heart more spirituality, a greater willingness to make sacrifices and a more practical Christian life. Learn from Him obedience to God and His representatives on earth and a great zeal for the honor of God. Learn from Him more patience in trials and tribulations; and lastly, learn from Him true humility and meekness of heart, charity toward your neighbor and greater forbearance in regard to his faults. Listen to what the beloved disciple writes: "Dearly beloved, let us love one another, for charity is of God. And everyone that loveth, is born of God, and knoweth God. He that loveth not, knoweth not God: for God is charity" (John 1: 7, 8).

C. *Christian soul, once you are filled with perfect love of God, you will feel a tender compassion for Jesus when you see how His love is often misjudged and even ridiculed.* Father Gallifet writes as follows: "The Heart of Jesus embraced mankind with an immeasurable love which has to enflame all hearts. But this infinite love is little heeded by men, most of them neglecting even to think of it. Yea, this hardheartedness and wickedness of men goes so far as to heap insults, indignities and blasphemies upon Jesus, their most benevolent benefactor, who dwells with us in the most Holy Sacrament. Who would not be most deeply affected by this conduct? Who would not desire to alleviate the pain which it thus caused the suffering Heart of Jesus, to repair the insults heaped upon It and to hold It in deep veneration?" From the revelations made to St. Margaret Mary, as well as from the utterances of bishops and popes, we must conclude that the aim of the devotion to the Sacred Heart is to make atonement and reparation for the ingratitude of men.

D. *The last and most sublime end of the devotion to the Sacred Heart is a perfect union of souls with Christ. This ideal was always the purpose of the Saviour, who made every sacrifice to obtain this final object.* All His thoughts, words and deeds, and every emotion of His Heart tended to achieve this great aim of His life, for the fulfillment of which He also offered His prayer as the divine High Priest. On that incomparable evening before His death, after the institution of the Holy Eucharist, in which He had given His disciples the final proof of His infinite love for them, He prayed: "Holy Father, keep them in Thy name whom Thou hast given Me; that they may be one, as We also are" (John 17:11). A moment later Jesus prayed thus: "Not for them only do I pray, but for them also who through their word shall believe in Me; that they all may be one, as Thou, Father, in Me, and I in Thee; that they also may be one in Us; that the world may believe that Thou hast sent Me . . . I in them, and Thou in Me; that they may be made perfect in one" (John 17:20 – 23). I have already shown that love is the chief motive, the very essence and aim, of the devotion to the Sacred Heart. But what is more likely to lead to love than a union of hearts? To be of one mind and one heart with Christ, to feel and think with Him, to be permeated by His spirit and to become more and more like Him by imitating His virtues: that is the final aim of the devotion to the Sacred Heart. St. Paul considers himself supremely happy because he has reached that goal. He writes to the Galatians: "And I live, now not I; but Christ liveth in me" (Gal. 2:20).

5. The Practice of the Devotion to the Sacred Heart

We distinguish between an exterior and an interior devotion to the Sacred Heart. The interior devotion is, of course, the more valuable; first, because it is necessary to the enlivening and the fructifying of the exterior devotion; secondly, because the inner life of the soul is enhanced and purified by devotion to the Sacred Heart. Sister Mary of the Sacred Heart (Countess Droste-Vischering), a favored follower of the Sacred Heart in modern times, relates that the Saviour informed her of His desire that the devotion to the Sacred Heart be propagated. He wished that now, since the revelations to St. Margaret Mary were better known, the interior devotion might grow.

A. The Interior Exercises of the Devotion to the Sacred Heart correspond to its aims

The principal ones are the following:
1. *Study the Heart of Jesus.* Procure the Gospels or a book on the life of Christ, and every day, or at least on Sundays and the First Fridays, read just one parable, or chapter.
2. *Love the Sacred Heart of Jesus.* Show a deep reverence and adoration to It. Admire, glorify and praise It. Thank Jesus Christ for His inexpressible goodness and love.
3. *Make reparation for the insults heaped upon the Heart of Jesus.* Do this not only in word but in deed as well, especially through works of mercy toward your neighbor, through self-denial and mortification, and finally through frequent reception of the Sacrament and adoration of the Blessed Sacrament.
4. *Unite yourself most intimately with the Heart of Jesus by the good intention to do all things out of love for Him.* Consecrate yourself entirely to the Sacred Heart. Make His interests your own. Let your only wish be that the divine Heart of Jesus be loved, glorified and praised by all people in the world.

B. Exterior Exercises of the Devotion to the Sacred Heart

Like every other devotion, devotion to the Sacred Heart has its exterior exercises. Some of these our Lord requested Margaret Mary to make public.
1. *The Feast of the Sacred Heart.* Its world-wide establishment and extension were closely related to the spread of the devotion to the Sacred Heart. This feast is now of the first class, and is celebrated on the Friday after the Octave of Corpus Christi. By order of Pope St. Pius X the Act of Consecration to the Sacred Heart as composed by Pope Leo XIII has been publicly recited in all Catholic churches for many years. The Act of Consecration as recited at the present time was issued by Pope Pius XI. This act is especially pleasing to Jesus, for He revealed to Margaret Mary: "I promised you that My Heart shall expand to shower gifts of My love upon all those who shall confer this honor upon Me." Therefore, Christian soul, if you wish to comply with the desire of your Saviour, you must prepare well for this Feast of the Sacred Heart, especially by meditation, perfect contrition and, if possible, a good confession; on the day itself receive Holy

Communion with fervent devotion and with the intention of making reparation for the insults which are committed against the Blessed Sacrament.

2. *The First Friday of every month is specially dedicated to the Heart of Jesus,* but of this phase of the devotion I shall treat later.

3. *The entire month of June is dedicated to the Sacred Heart, the feast itself usually falling within this month.* You should sanctify this whole month by daily prayer before an image of the Sacred Heart, or at least by attending the public devotions in your parish church.

4. *All the adorers of the Sacred Heart are urged to use the indulgenced prayers authorized by the Church.* Among these are the Novena and Litany of the Sacred Heart. Try to memorize ejaculations to the Sacred Heart, so that you may consecrate to It every hour of the day.

5. *It is understood, of course, that adorers of the Sacred Heart also revere pictures of this most holy Heart.* It is the earnest desire of the Saviour that the picture of His most Sacred Heart be exposed in all churches and homes in order that men may be more readily reminded of His love. Certainly you should not make a haphazard choice of a picture of the Sacred Heart. A picture which represents such a sublime subject must, first of all, have merit. Representations of the Heart only, without the figure of our dear Saviour, are still tolerated by the Church for private devotion, but are not to be recommended. The approved pictures represent the Saviour in the noble dignity of His loving humanity, pointing with one hand to His Heart, inflamed with love, which is visible on His breast.

6. *Every adorer of the Sacred Heart will endeavor to belong to the League of the Sacred Heart, which is known as the Apostleship of Prayer.*

7. *The Perpetual Adoration of the Sacred Heart of Jesus.* The Missionaries of the Sacred Heart instituted this Confraternity on March 26, 1874, in the Church of Our Lady of the Sacred Heart in Rome. It was raised to an Archconfraternity as early as June 26 of the same year. Wherever it is feasible, the members unite in groups of seven or eight, each person undertaking to perform one of

the seven principal acts of devotion to the Sacred Heart on the appointed days. These acts are: adoration, love, thanksgiving, petition, compassion, expiation and union.

8. *The Sacred Heart Missionary Crusade.* The aim of the Sacred Heart Missionary Crusade is to spread everywhere devotion to the Sacred Heart in accordance with the revelations made to St. Margaret Mary, and to educate young men for the priesthood as Missionaries of the Sacred Heart, trained to do missionary work at home and abroad. This Missionary Crusade was approved and recommended by the Popes Pius IX, Pius X, Benedict XV and Pius XI, as well as by many archbishops and bishops. Pope Benedict XV granted to all benefactors a special Apostolic Blessing at the hour of death. The main office of the Sacred Heart Missionary Crusade is at the Sacred Heart Monastery, 305 South Lake Street, Aurora, Illinois.

6. The Blessings of the Devotion to the Sacred Heart

In this small volume it is impossible to describe the imposing history of the many blessings showered upon mankind since the beginning of the devotion to the Sacred Heart: sinners have been converted; many poor, afflicted, distressed and exiled souls have been comforted; countless others have been led to great sanctity: convents and religious institutions have been inspired to a renewed practice of virtue; yes, even entire nations have been greatly benefited by this devotion. We find a partial record of these blessings in the literature of the past and the present; the complete record, however, shall be known to us only in eternity, in the happy Kingdom of the Heart of Jesus. There is no doubt that the promises contained in the revelations made to St. Margaret Mary have been fulfilled in the past and will be fulfilled in time to come. The greatest of these revelations is: "Proclaim this, and let it be proclaimed throughout the entire world: I will assign no measure and no limit to the gifts and graces which I will bestow on all who seek them in My Heart."

In the letters and other writings of St. Margaret Mary we find many promises which Jesus made to her. The principal ones are:
1. I will give them all the graces necessary for their state in life.
2. I will give them peace in their families.

3. I will comfort them in all their afflictions.
4. I will be their secure refuge during life and especially at the hour of death.
5. I will bestow abundant blessings upon all their undertakings.
6. Sinners shall find in My Heart a source and boundless ocean of mercy.
7. Tepid souls shall become fervent.
8. Fervent souls shall advance rapidly to high perfection.
9. I will bless the houses in which an image of My Sacred Heart shall be set up and honored.
10. I will give the priests the power of touching the most hardened hearts.
11. Persons who spread this devotion shall have their names written in my Heart, never to be effaced.

Part II: The First Fridays of the Sacred Heart

From the writings of St. Margaret Mary it is not clear whether our Lord desired the observance of the First Friday to become as general as the celebration of the Feast of the Sacred Heart. At first He requested this devotion of her alone. She tells us: "My divine Saviour requested me to communicate on the First Friday of every month in order to make reparation as much as was in my power, for the disrespect offered to the Blessed Sacrament during the previous month." Who would dare to say that this request was not meant for all lovers of the Sacred Heart?

St. Margaret Mary made every effort, therefore, to introduce the observance of the First Fridays into convents and even among the laity. She recommends especially the reception of Holy Communion and the consecration to the Sacred Heart. The essential practice of the First Fridays has always been reparation for the sins committed against the offended, blasphemed and neglected Heart of the Eucharistic God.

Pope Leo XIII praised this devotion and recommended it to all people, granting special indulgences and privileges to those who practice it. He allowed a solemn Votive Mass in honor of the Sacred Heart on that day, and granted a plenary indulgence to the members of the Apostleship of Prayer, to be gained on the First Friday of every month under the usual conditions of Confession, Holy Communion and prayer for the intention of the Pope, together with a short meditation on the infinite goodness of the Sacred Heart.

What has thus far been said pertains to the exterior devotion to the Sacred Heart on the First Friday of every month, which includes the following exercises: Communion of Reparation, atonement and consecration.

It would certainly be of little avail to practice only the exterior devotion without entering into its spirit. The Communion of Reparation, for example, will be a true act of reparation only if you receive with all possible fervor, love, contrition, humility and resignation. In like manner, the acts of atonement will please our Lord much more if, on this day, you consider more fully His goodness and love, and endeavor to unite your heart more closely to His own. The devout observance of the First Friday, therefore, constitutes, as it were, a monthly spiritual renovation of your heart and soul.

The Great Promise

Dear reader, the amazing revelation of which I now desire to speak to you is not taken from the Bible nor from tradition; neither is it a dogma of the Church. For its truth we depend on the writings of St. Margaret Mary. But you realize how wonderfully she was favored by the Sacred Heart and how humble, modest and obedient she remained in spite of the revelations which Jesus had made to her. These revelations she made known in obedience to her superiors.

During the month of May, in the year 1688, she wrote to her superior in Dijon: "During Holy Communion on a certain Friday the Lord spoke to me, His unworthy servant, the following words: 'I promise thee in the excessive mercy of My Heart that My all-powerful love will grant to all those who communicate on the First Friday in nine consecutive months the grace of final penitence; they shall not die in My disgrace nor without having received the sacraments; My Divine Heart shall be their safe refuge at that last moment.'"

This has rightly been called the Great Promise. I shall tell you the reason why. Many are filled with fear at the thought of death. How shall I die? Shall I die suddenly, without preparation, contrition, or the sacraments? How easy it is to relapse into sin and to die impenitent! Many a one has asked himself these questions in fear, and has recalled the warning of the Apostle to work out our salvation in fear and trembling. Do not be discouraged, dear reader. A ray of hope, coming from the Heart of Jesus, dispels this gloomy feeling and the torturing uncertainty with regard to your last hour. Your Saviour promises you the grace of final repentance.

We are treating here of the most precious gift of grace that can be granted to sinful man, namely, the grace of a happy death. It is really a spiritual business transaction, a sort of insurance for eternity. The premium and the conditions of the contract are clearly stated. You must receive Holy Communion worthily on the First Friday of nine consecutive months. A necessary condition, of course, is this, that you receive with a pure intention and with the firm resolution to serve your Saviour faithfully throughout your life and never to offend Him by mortal sin. The mental reservation, "Oh, I can sin again later on," would be blasphemous and make your Communion sacrilegious. Moreover, the Lord would not be hold to His promise; on the contrary, you would have greater reason to fear for your salvation. Here I wish to state also that the promise of our Lord must be understood literally, that is, the Holy Communion must be received on the First Fridays and not on the following Sunday. It is true that you may receive the same indulgences on the first Sunday of the month, because the Church is free to use her power of the keys as she wishes; but she cannot change the word of God. For the same reason the sequence of the Communions may not be broken. Should you be obliged to miss one First Friday, you would have to begin all over again.

Dear reader, do not allow scruples to restrain you from making this novena of grace. It promises you that you shall remain in the state of grace, and should you be so unfortunate as to fall into mortal sin again, it promises you the grace of final repentance.

This novena is bound to have a powerful effect on your entire life and is therefore highly recommended. It will not only save but also sanctify your soul. The time will come when you will thank the divine Heart of Jesus, the fountain of all grace, for having given this bountiful promise and thus aided you to gain a glorious and everlasting crown.

FIRST FRIDAY IN JANUARY

Heart of Jesus, substantially united to the Word of God, have mercy on us.

"In the beginning was the Word, and the Word was with God, and the Word was God." (John 1:1)

Meditation

God has spoken to man in many ways. Behold the heavens with innumerable stars so far away that we poor mortals have no conception of their incredible speed and cannot hear the rush and roar as they pass through space. Nevertheless, these soundless heavens are like a vast parchment on which is written a word of the Creator's power, glory and goodness. "The heavens proclaim the glory of God." This is also true of the earth and all created things: the mountains, valleys, rivers, seas, plants, animals and – man. Let this thought sink deep into your soul: you are a word of God, an image and likeness of the Creator.

God has spoken to man in a still more wonderful manner. He descended from the heavenly heights into Paradise and spoke with Adam and Eve. On Mount Sinai He proclaimed His laws amid thunder and lightening and the sound of trumpets. Later on He spoke to the Israelites through His only-begotten Son, Jesus Christ. This last Word of God is the most glorious of all. St. John speaks of Him when he begins his gospel with these words: "In the beginning was the Word, and the Word was with God, and the Word was God."

The visible world and everything that is good, beautiful and sublime is a word, spoken by God since the beginning of time. Jesus Christ, however, is the original and very own Word of God from all eternity, as infinite as the Father, eternal, almighty, omniscient and infinitely holy. He is as truly God as the Father. Even as your thoughts emanate from your mind and yet remain there, so, too, but in a much more mysterious manner, the Word (that is, the Son) proceeds from the Father and yet remains united with Him. The Father and the Son are united in a love which is incomprehensible and eternal; and as you take delight in your own thoughts, so the heavenly Father finds unlimited joy in His Word, His only-begotten Son.

Take heed, my soul, and adore! Adore the Word of the eternal Father. Kneel in the dust of the earth before the infinite Wisdom of God!

Everything that God has created He has created by His Word. All light, warmth and life come from Him. He is the true Light which enlightens your heart and your soul; it is the very life through which, in faith, we are reborn children of God.

Rejoice, my soul, and hear the most sublime message of the New Law: "And the Word was made flesh, and dwelt amongst us." The second divine Person became man, uniting Himself with human flesh and blood and with a created human soul in the womb of the Virgin Mary. The eternal Wisdom and Love of God became a child: "This shall be a sign unto you: You shall find the Infant wrapped in swaddling clothes, lying in a manger" (Luke 2:12). Hasten to the stable at Bethlehem and adore this Word of God. Fear not, because It is but a poor, helpless Child; and It is so lovable, so dear and beautiful in Its poverty. See how benignly It looks upon you and how tenderly It extends Its hand toward you! It most assuredly has a Heart for you. Oh, adore this Heart of the Infant Jesus which is inseparably united to the Word of God forever and ever. It is the Heart of your God.

The eternal Father created everything through the power of His word, and in like manner, the Word, the only-begotten Son of God, will do nothing without first consulting His Heart. Yea, henceforth all the plans and decrees of God will first be weighed and approved by this Heart. From the fullness of this Heart we shall all receive, grace upon grace.

Furthermore, this Heart is the most docile of all hearts. God the Father does not find in any other heart so much love, loyalty and submission as in the Heart of His divine Son; no other heart glorifies and adores the Father so constantly; no other heart imitates Him so perfectly as this Heart which is substantially united with His eternal Word. The Heart of Jesus proclaims the glory of God more than all creation, visible and invisible. "And we have seen His glory, the glory of the only-begotten of the Father, full of grace and truth."

My soul, would you not wish to be united with God even as the Heart of Jesus is united with the Word of God? Then you must be pure of heart as He is, and your thoughts and desires must be in perfect harmony with His. Nothing sinful must be allowed to stain your soul, and you must be of one mind with Christ.

DEVOTION FOR COMMUNION

You are convinced, Christian soul, that your divine Savior is really and truly present in the Blessed Sacrament; you also know that His loving Heart desires to be united with you; your faith sets forth the wealth of grace that is contained in this Sacrament; it teaches you that the Saviour has pledged eternal life to those who eat His Flesh and drink His Blood; you also know that no authority on earth can forbid you to partake of this Food for souls; as regards your rights to receive Holy Communion, you have only one judge, namely, God, who speaks through your conscience. Pope Pius X solemnly declared that you have an undisputed right to receive Holy Communion daily. Therefore, why do you hesitate? Why neglect this necessary Food for souls and manifest such coldness toward your Saviour? Christian soul, make this First Friday of the year a day of heart-felt resolution, a turning point in your life. You wish to be a true follower of Christ; resolve, therefore, to receive Holy Communion at least every month. Should you be able to receive oftener, then be generous in your proofs of love toward the magnanimous Heart of Jesus.

BEFORE HOLY COMMUNION

Faith and Adoration
O Thou most blessed Word of God, Thou true reflection of the eternal Father, Thou most sublime Son in whom the Father is well pleased, I believe in Thy real presence in the Blessed Sacrament. With deepest reverence I adore Thee, before whom the seraphim are enraptured and all the choirs of angels tremble in blissful ecstasy. In all humility I cast myself down before Thy hidden Majesty. It is true that my eyes do not see Thee, but I know that Thou art the light which dispels all darkness; Thou art the true light which enlightens everyone who receives Thee. Thou didst become man that all might learn to know Thee. Through Thee the goodness and benevolence of God have

become manifest to man. Whoever sees Thee, sees also the Father. Thou hast taken to Thyself a Heart and adorned It with the most magnificent gifts and virtues. It is Thy Heart, substantially united with Thee, worthy of adoration even as Thou art.

O most Sacred Heart of Jesus, with the deepest conviction of my faith I confess Thy divine dignity and adore Thee as the Heart of my God. O Divine Heart, really and truly present on this altar under the form of bread, Thou burning bush, from which the voice of the heavenly Father declared: "Put off the shoes from thy feet: for the place whereon thou standest is holy ground" (Exod. 3:5). Increase in me the faith in Thy real presence. Refine and purify me in the fire of Thy zeal, that my heart may become, even as Thine own, an altar of sacrifice for the honor and glory of the heavenly Father.

Hope

O Jesus, who once didst say: "I am the light of the world: he that followeth Me, walketh not in darkness" (John 8:12), behold, I place my whole confidence in Thy gentle kindness. Thou art my light, my star of hope, my guide in this vale of darkness and confusion. The image of Thy Heart, enflamed with love for me, fills my heart with hope and confidence, even as the light of dawn rejoices the heart of man as the forerunner of a glorious day. I hope and pray that a ray of that glory which is Thine with the eternal Father may enter into my poor, sinful heart, so that I may follow Thee with courage here on earth and be blessed with the vision of Thy divine Heart in heaven.

Love

O sweetest Jesus, Thou didst come to bring fire into this loveless world and Thou dost earnestly desire that this fire be enkindled. O my Saviour, Thou couldst not restrain the flames of Thy love for us, and therefore Thou didst open Thy breast to reveal Thy infinite love to all men. Enkindle the fire of Thy love in my heart also. Oh, give me a heart as generous as Thine so that I may be prepared for every sacrifice. Out of love for me Thou didst once take unto Thyself a human nature and didst become a poor and helpless child; out of love for me Thou, the eternal Wisdom and Love, Thou, the glorious Word of God, didst institute this Blessed Sacrament although thereby Thou didst expose Thyself to the danger of being insulted and neglected by me, a sinful creature. O my Jesus, from the bottom of my heart I declare myself prepared to make reparation for my own sins as well as for those of all mankind. I joyfully give Thee a small token of my love today by consecrating myself entirely to Thee in Holy Communion. Oh, do Thou with me as Thou willest.

"Sweet Heart of Jesus, make me love Thee ever more and more." (Indulgence: 300 days. Plenary once a month if said every day.)

Humility and Contrition

O Jesus, at the thought of my unworthiness I should draw away from Thy divine Majesty. How is it possible that I, a creature, who have so often disfigured the image of God in my soul by my sins, dare to approach Thy altar and constrain Thee to enter my soul? But, my Jesus, didst Thou not urgently invite the weary and the hungry, namely, the sinners, to come to Thee? Didst Thou not solemnly declare that Thou hadst come not for the sake of the just but for sinners, that they may have life in abundance? Yea, Thy loving Heart does not reject even the most wretched sinner who comes to Thee with a contrite heart.

Again I repent and lament all the sins of my whole life because through them I have so deeply wounded Thy most Sacred Heart. Especially do I bemoan my former coldness toward Thee, my irreverence in Thy presence in the Blessed Sacrament, my distractions during the Holy Sacrifice of the Mass, my lukewarmness in the reception of Thy most precious Flesh and Blood.

"My Jesus, mercy." (Indulgence: 300 days. Plenary once a month if said every day.)

"Eucharistic Heart of Jesus, have mercy on us." (Indulgence: 300 days.)

After Holy Communion

Remember that there are no more precious hours in life than those immediately following Holy Communion. Then you are united in the most sublime manner with the Word of God; then you are heart to heart with Him. The angels enjoy no greater privilege in heaven than you at the Table of the Lord, because even in heaven they cannot be more intimately united with God. There is but one difference: they see God face to face, and you see Him through faith. But did not the Apostle say that faith is a compensation for sight and knowledge? And did not the Lord declare them blessed who believe without seeing? Enjoy, therefore, to the full these short minutes of heavenly happiness. Before using your prayer book, let your heart alone speak to Jesus in fervent, mental prayer.

Thanksgiving

My soul doth magnify the Lord, and my spirit rejoiceth in God my Saviour, because He hath regarded the humility of His servant. He descended from the heights of heaven and chose the lowliest among His creatures in order to enlighten it with the brilliancy of His divinity and to enrich it, out of the fullness of His Heart, with grace upon grace. O infinite love of my God, I adore Thee from the innermost depths of my heart; I praise and glorify Thee; I thank Thee for this greatest of all favors. Far be it from me, henceforth to glory in aught but Thee; Thou art my life and my all! Thou in me, and I in Thee! Oh, do not permit me ever to desire anything else but Thee; grant that I may possess only Thee; Thou art sufficient for me. Abide with me, most Sacred Heart of Jesus, and may my heart be as intimately united with Thine as Thou art united with the Word of the eternal Father. May the bond of love with which Thou hast this day drawn me to Thyself keep me ever close to Thy Heart.

Petition

O my Jesus, Thou hast loved me from all eternity. Thou hast manifested Thy love through Thy Incarnation and Birth. Unto Thy very death Thou didst give proof of Thy infinite love for Thy Apostles, and through them, for me also, by instituting this most precious remembrance of Thy Passion and Death. By the most sacred wound in Thy Heart I conjure Thee, my sweetest Jesus, to pierce my heart with the fire of Thy love; wound me so deeply that to heal me will be forever impossible. Oh, that I could truthfully say: "I live, now not I, but Christ liveth in me."

But oh, how can I speak to Thee with such presumption

when I consider my former Communions and the many holy resolutions which I neglected to keep? Do not, O merciful Jesus, remember my unfaithfulness, but remember only Thy mercy and love. Prove Thy infinite forbearance with a creature who can be faithful only with the help of Thy grace. Help me! Spur me on to fidelity toward Thee, not only now when Thou art substantially present in my heart, but also when the sweet odor of Thy presence has departed from my soul and the healing effect of Thy living Heart has diminished. When the temptations of the world, sensuality, pride and self-love afflict me, then remind me, O Jesus, of the holy resolutions which I have made, and grant me the courage to remain true to Thee.

Note: Call to mind your principal fault and the occasions which have led you into sin in the past. Resolve to avoid these occasions so that you will not again be overcome by temptation. Then recite the following prayers:

"Sweet Heart of Jesus, I implore, that I may love Thee more and more."

"My Jesus, for Thee I live; my Jesus, for Thee I die; my Jesus, I am Thine in life and in death."

"Most sacred and loving Heart of Jesus, fountain of all graces, give me Thy blessing. May this Thy blessing give me courage in time of temptation, and perseverance in my good resolutions. Abide with me until the last day of my life."

Offering

O Lord Jesus Christ, in union with that divine intention with which Thou didst on earth offer praises to God through Thy Sacred Heart, and now dost continue to offer them in all places in the Sacrament of the Eucharist, and wilt do so to the end of the world, I most willingly offer Thee, through this entire day without the smallest exception, all my intentions and thoughts, all my affections and desires, all my words and actions, that they may be conformed to the most sacred heart of the Blessed Virgin Mary, ever Immaculate. (Indulgence: 3 years once a day. Plenary once a month if said every day.)

Reparation to the Sacred Heart of Jesus

O Sacred Heart of Jesus, Thou hast lavished Thy blessings upon men, and yet most of them scorn Thy favors and despise the wonderful gifts of Thy goodness.

Sinners outrage Thee, the indifferent forsake Thee; and, alas, even pious souls neglect Thee by their frequent lack of fervor and respect. The very ones for whom Thy Eucharistic love is intended in a special way ignore and offend Thee. Therefore, kneeling before Thy altar, we wish to repair, by special homage, the heinous outrages with which men everywhere wound Thy love.

Oh, that we could compensate Thee for them and could console Thee by greater love for the neglect, the insults, and the wicked contempt shown toward Thee. Deign, then, to accept this offering of our reparation in union with the satisfaction rendered Thee by the Virgin Mary, the saints, and all pious and faithful souls.

O Sacred Heart of Jesus, forgive Thy wandering, guilty children. And in Thy goodness pour forth Thy mercy upon them and upon us, we beseech Thee, through the Immaculate Heart of Mary, our dearest Mother. Amen.

Our Lady of the Sacred Heart, pray for us.

St. Joseph, model and patron of those who love the Sacred Heart of Jesus, pray for us.

FIRST FRIDAY IN FEBRUARY

Heart of Jesus, in whom the Father is well pleased, have mercy on us.

"This is my beloved Son in whom I am well pleased." (Matt. 3: 17)

Meditation

On a certain night centuries ago, a brilliant light illuminated the plains near Bethlehem, and a messenger from heaven appeared to the watching shepherds and said: "Behold, I bring you tidings of great joy … for this day is born to you a Saviour, who is Christ the Lord, in the city of David. And this shall be a sign unto you: you shall find the Infant wrapped in swaddling clothes, and laid in a manger" (Luke 2:10-12). The angel had hardly ceased to speak, when "suddenly there was with him a multitude of the heavenly army, praising God and saying: 'Glory to God in the highest; and on earth peace to men of good will.'"

What was the wonderful event that caused the heavenly spirits to descend to earth? Why do they appear to these poor shepherds on the plains? What kind of feast for the poor and humble can this indeed really be, that heaven and earth meet in a kiss of peace?

Is it possible? Is this child, born in a stable, wrapped in swaddling clothes and laid in a manger, truly the Son of God? Can it be that this Son of the Almighty is to be recognized by His very poverty and frailty? Is that the honor which is to be given to the heavenly Father? And is this poverty and frailty the reason that the angels sing: "Glory to God in the highest?"

Here is certainly a strange conception of honor and one such as is not customary among men. If the Son of God really desired to become man to prove His divine love for us, should not His heavenly Father have provided the most beautiful place in all the world for His habitation? But instead of doing that, Almighty God permitted Him to be born in a lowly stable, chose for Him poor parents, did not even grant Him a hut for Himself, suffered Him, even in His childhood, to endure the greatest privations, contempt, persecution and exile, and finally sent Him to a poor dwelling in Nazareth. God the Father willed that His Son live there in seclusion until He reach the age of thirty years, and be generally considered the Son of a carpenter.

In this manner does God rear, if I may use the expression, His only-begotten Son in humility and seems even proud to have a Son who is misjudged and despised by men. And it is precisely because His Son obeys with such willingness and submission, that the heavenly Father publicly professes His great pleasure in this Son, when, on the occasion of His baptism in the Jordan, He said: "This is My beloved Son, in whom I am well pleased." The Father who is in heaven judges differently from earthly fathers. The latter show too much interest in the outward appearance, the natural talent and advantages of their children. The heavenly Father looks into the Heart of Jesus and there He sees a Heart filled with perfect filial love, greater than any He receives from the children of men.

From the first moment of the Incarnation, at His birth in the stable at Bethlehem, during His exile in Egypt and during His life at Nazareth, the Heart and mind of Jesus were in closest union with the divine Father. Even as a child Jesus knew no other will but the will of His heavenly Father. "All that is Mine is Thine ... not My will but Thine be done." Thus Jesus prayed without ceasing. Consider His words and actions in the temple, the house of His Father. There He feels so perfectly at home that His Heart is ever drawn to it. At the age of twelve He seems untouched by the sorrow He caused His beloved Mother, so that when she asked Him, "Son, why hast Thou done so to us?" He answers: "Did you not know that I must be about my Father's business?" As much as to say: "Where the honor of my heavenly Father is concerned, I have no consideration for flesh and blood."

These same words might well be written on the door of the tabernacle, because they are the key to a better understanding of the sublime mystery of the perpetual presence of Jesus. In fact, He lives in the tabernacle, where His Heart beats continually in honor of His heavenly Father, while, day after day and hour after hour, men disobey the will of the eternal God. Outside the tabernacle there is a constant struggle for earthly goods, for honor and reputation and sensual pleasures; but, thanks be to God! Here in the tabernacle there beats a Heart in solitude, repeating: "Not My will but Thine be done." The loving Heart of Jesus yearns to remain poor, hidden and humble, in order to atone for the pride of the world and to restore the honor of God.

Could it be possible that the divine Father would not be pleased with the heroic Heart of His Son? For those who have ears to hear, the words of the Father are heard again as they were heard on the banks of the Jordan and on Mount Tabor: "This is my beloved Son in whom I am well pleased."

My soul, from the Heart of Jesus you, too, must learn complete submission to the holy will of God. You, too, must work zealously for the glory of God. It is not necessary for you to perform extraordinary deeds. It matters not whether you are honored or admired by others; the important thing is that God be honored, loved and adored. Follow the example of the Heart of Jesus in the tabernacle: offer yourself to God every day and hour; perform your daily duties, the lowliest as well as the important ones, without thinking of any other reward but the friendship and love of the Heart of Jesus, your Brother. United your intentions with His, and you may have confidence that in you also the Father will be pleased.

PRAYERS FOR HOLY COMMUNION

Every Holy Communion should be received for a special intention. The purpose of the Communion on the First Friday should always be reparation to the Sacred Heart of Jesus for the sinfulness of men. This need not hinder you from adding your own personal intention which may be of value to your soul.

BEFORE HOLY COMMUNION

Prayer to God the Father

Eternal Father, Thou first cause of all sanctity, Thou inexpressible fountain of wisdom, from whom Thy only-begotten and well-beloved Son proceed, how dare I, a poor sinner, approach to receive Thy Son? The very thought that Jesus is Thy Son fills me with holy fear. I am reminded of His humility and submission whenever He spoke of Thee. I remember the boundless devotedness which He manifested toward Thee from the first moment of His life on earth until His death on the cross: "Father, into Thy hands I commend My spirit." How, then, can I dare to approach Him? Does He not belong entirely to Thee? Did He Himself not say: "All that is Mine is Thine. Not My will but Thine be done?"

However, I have one consolation. Thou art particularly pleased by Thy divine Son's humility and deliberate self-abnegation, through which He became like unto me except in sin. I am comforted by Thy word: "Hear ye Him." And what does Thy Son say to me? Oh, He teaches me that His Father is also my Father, that I, a miserable creature and only a prodigal son, am nevertheless a child of His Father. O benevolent Father of my Saviour. Thou willest even now to be my Father; Thou desirest to adopt me as Thy son. From the bottom of my Heart I pray that I, too, may be Thy beloved son.

"Eternal Father, by the most precious Blood of Jesus Christ, glorify His most holy name according to the intention and desires of His adorable Heart." (Indulgence: 300 days when said as reparation for blasphemies against the Most Holy Name of Jesus. Plenary once a month if said every day.)

Sweetest Jesus, Thou didst come into this world to glorify Thy heavenly Father and to restore anew His kingdom among men. God and souls! These were the object of Thy life; for this Thou didst yearn and labor, to make all men children of God. This was the ambition of Thy Heart, the Heart of the Son of God, and of my Brother as well. But how strange do Thy ways seem to me! For thirty years Thou didst remain hidden and misjudged, and only for three years didst Thou work in public. How different are Thy ways from my ways and Thy thoughts from my thoughts! I praise and thank Thee for the glory Thou hast given to Thy heavenly Father by Thy hidden life. Grant me the grace to emulate Thy example. Preserve me from the evil influences of the world, from the spirit of pride and self-aggrandizement, and through this Holy Communion admit me to the safe refuge of Thy Sacred Heart. The remembrance of many grievous sins, especially the thought of my ingratitude, through which I have pained Thee so much, causes deep sorrow and shame in my soul. Indeed, after having forsaken Thy Father so often, I am not worthy to call Thee my Brother; but do Thou speak only a word to Thy Father, and I shall have hope of being adopted once more by His grace.

Prayer to Mary for Purity of Heart

O Mary, Mother of my Saviour, do thou accept me as thy child; protect me in my weakness with the mantle of thy motherly love. Recommend me to thy Son and place me under His care. O thou treasurer of the Heart of Jesus, our Lady of the Sacred Heart, draw thou from the depths of this Heart the treasures of Its graces and enrich my heart with them. Through thy intercession with Jesus, thy Son, obtain for me the special grace to receive this Holy Communion with perfect purity of heart, so that it may be the pledge of my eternal salvation.

Faith, Hope and Charity

O Lord Jesus Christ, I firmly believe that Thou art the true Son of God and of Mary. I profess an unswerving faith in the infinite value of the atonement which Thou didst render to Thy heavenly Father from the first moment of Thy earthly existence until Thy baptism in the Jordan, through Thy obedience, poverty, humility and complete abandonment to the will of Thy Father; I also believe that Thou doest make atonement in an even more incomprehensible manner by Thy presence in the tabernacle. This I truly believe because Thy Father in heaven has given testimony of it at the Jordan.

I hope with confidence to be accepted as Thy child and to be an heir of heaven, because Thou hast merited these favors for me by Thy childlike obedience.

Oh, that I could love Thee always with all my heart and be consumed with love for Thee. My most beloved Jesus, help me to love Thee not only in words but also in deed and in truth.

"Sweet Heart of Jesus, be my love." (Indulgence: 300 days.)

Desire

The moment approaches when the Son of God will enter my heart to bestow upon me, a poor sinner, the most inexplicable honor that is bestowed on a child of God on earth. Be astonished, ye choirs of angels, at the sight of a lowly creature being thus favored; and since you cannot partake of this divine Food, inflame my poor heart with a burning love of God, so that I may desire nothing but the possession of this Spouse of souls and that I may never again be separated from Him. Come, then, my Jesus, my Brother; sanctify, strengthen and purify me, so that the Father may be well pleased with me.

"Sacred Heart of Jesus, I trust in Thee." (Indulgence: 300 days. Plenary once a month.)

AFTER HOLY COMMUNION

Meditate for a few moments upon the wonderful favor which has been bestowed upon you, and dwell especially on the thought that now you are "one heart and one soul" with the Son of God, and that your Jesus is with you. After this meditation greet the Heart of your Brother most reverently, and through It give whole-hearted thanks to God the Father.

Offering to the Heavenly Father

Most loving Father, look benignly upon Thy poor creature who now enjoys the presence of Thy beloved Son within his heart. Now Jesus lives within me. He who was begotten of Thee from all eternity, before the stars were created, has become my very own through Thy grace even as He is ever Thine by nature. This, Thy Son, in whom Thou art well pleased, I now embrace, as once the faithful Simeon embraced Him in the temple. Behold, I offer Him to Thee even as in childhood He offered Himself in the temple. From Thy throne, O loving Father, look favorably upon this my gift. It is Thy true Son, who became man and lay in the manger as a poor helpless child, and who during His whole life remained in poverty. This Thy Son it is whom I offer to Thee in acknowledgment of the almighty power and glory with which Thou dost rule all creatures. I offer Him to Thee as Thine eternal joy and delight; I offer Him as a complete compensation for all the favors which flow upon all earthly and celestial beings; I offer Him to Thee as an abounding atonement for all the ignominy which has been heaped on Thee by Thy ungrateful creatures; I offer Him to Thee for an increase of celestial bliss for all Thy elect, especially for the Blessed Virgin Mary, my guardian angel and my patron saint. I offer Him to Thee for my parents, brothers and sisters, friends and benefactors, for N. N. .... and for all those who have recommended themselves to my prayers. Furthermore, I offer Him to Thee that He may love, praise and thank Thee for all the blessings which Thou hast bestowed on me from the time of my creation unto this very hour, and also that He may make fitting reparation for all my faults and sins. Lastly, my most loving Father, I offer Him to Thee for the poor souls in Purgatory, particularly for those for whom I am in duty bound to pray. In the name of Thy beloved Son grant their desire to behold Thy face and permit them to enter into the mansions which Thou hast prepared for them, that they may enjoy Thy beatific vision throughout all eternity. Amen.

Indulgenced Prayer to the Sacred Heart
O Divine Heart of Jesus, grant, we beseech Thee, eternal rest to the souls in purgatory, the final grace of salvation to those who shall die today, true repentance to sinners, the light of faith to pagans, and Thy blessing to me and mine. To Thee O most compassionate Heart of Jesus, I commend all these souls; and I offer to Thee on their behalf all Thy merits together with the merits of Thy most holy Mother and of all the saints and angels, and all the holy Masses, Communions, prayers and good works which shall be offered today throughout the Christian world.
(Indulgence: 500 days each time.)

Resolution
O my sweetest Jesus, now that I belong to Thee alone, do not permit me ever to be separated from Thee. Fortify my heart against all temptations of the flesh and the seductions of this godless world. Remove from my heart every inclination forward the forbidden fruits of this fleeting life, and grant me instead a hunger and thirst for Thy love and friendship. O Thou, my divine Friend, aid me in making a holy covenant with Thee, sealed with the blood of Thy Sacred Heart. Henceforth I desire to seek only Thy honor and to propagate the love of Thy most Sacred Heart. May Thy loving Heart be known, praised, glorified, loved and adored everywhere and at all times. In this solemn moment I promise to Thy Sacred Heart my love and loyalty unto death. I declare myself willing to fulfill Thy every wish. Because I know that deeds are more pleasing to Thee than words I promise to practice the following virtue today. (Mention some special act, such as almsgiving, kindness, forgiveness, etc.) Moreover, I promise to be particularly steadfast in combating my principal fault during this month, and for this purpose to

examine my conscience every evening. But do Thou, O sweetest Jesus, have patience with me if I become forgetful of my promise; Thou knowest how weak I am. Only in Thee and with Thy grace shall I be able to keep my resolution.

"Heart of Jesus, burning with love of us, inflame our hearts with love of Thee." (Indulgence: 500 days. Plenary once a month if said every day.)

Prayer to the Divine Heart of Jesus

O Jesus, Thou didst once labor and suffer unto the exhaustion of Thy strength to give men the most wonderful and irrefutable proofs of Thy inexhaustible love for them, and yet these ungrateful creatures have rewarded Thee with only ingratitude. Even in our times Thou dost burn for love of us in the Blessed Sacrament, and still men are indifferent toward Thee. I am deeply grieved because of the insults and offenses offered to Thee in this Sacrament of Thy love, and I humbly cast myself into the dust before Thy Sacred Heart to ask Thy pardon. I detest the sin of ingratitude, of which I feel so guilty, and also the neglect which I have shown Thee. I also detest and abhor the sins and sacrileges which others have committed against Thee. Through this my voluntary submission and atonement I desire to repair the sins committed against the reverence due to Thee.

Oh, that I could atone for all the misdeeds of men by the shedding of my tears and my blood! Oh, that I could expiate, by extraordinary reverence, all the outrages and sacrileges committed in the past! How happy would I be if I could give my life for such a just cause! Pardon me, my sweet Jesus, and strengthen my will by Thy grace. In the future, with the help of Thy grace, I will strive with all my strength never to be found negligent in the reverence and love which I owe Thee. I am determined to repair my former irreverence by adoration, my indifference by sacrifice, and my lukewarmness by love. Grant me Thy grace, O Jesus, that I may keep my resolution. Amen.

FIRST FRIDAY IN MARCH

Heart of Jesus, bruised for our offenses, have mercy on us.

"My soul is sorrowful even unto death: stay you here and watch with me." (Matt. 26:38)

Meditation

Sin is the greatest of all evils. Because of sin the earth is dreary and desolate, and many hearts feel destitute of all joy. The Heart of Jesus is sorrowful unto death, because the sins of man inundate His Father's glorious creation like and ocean of slime and offal.

Look upon Him, Christian soul, during His agony in the Garden of Olives. Oh, what change do we see in Him! Vanished is the sublime and solemn peace with which He used to pray to His heavenly Father; His body shudders; indescribable loathing fills His Heart; He gazes upward to His eternal Father. But alas! He who once said: "This is my beloved Son, in whom I am well pleased," is now wrapped in profound silence. A dark, impenetrable veil hides from the pleading Son of Man the countenance of His heavenly Father, at other times so ravishing. The words of Isaias are being fulfilled: "In a moment of indignation have I hid My face … from thee." "Your iniquities have divided between you and your God, and your sins have hid His face from you that He should not hear" (Isaias 54:8 and 59:2).

O horrible sins! They weigh heavily upon His Heart. At this moment, He sees the sins of man in all their hideousness. He alone must bear the guilt of these sins because it is written: "The Lord hath laid on Him the iniquity of us all" (Isaias 53:6). He is the only sinner accountable before God; His is the only one culpable, He who has never grieved the heavenly Father. A terrible fear overpowers Him, and His soul becomes sorrowful unto death. A groan of horror escapes from His lips as He calls upon His Father: "Father, if it be possible, let this chalice pass from Me" (Matt. 26:39). Let them come, Judas the traitor and the mob; let them scoff and deliver Me into the hands of cruel pagans to be scourged and crucified – Thy holy will be done! One thing only I ask of Thee – remove from My shoulders the terrible weight of sin, its guilt. Take from these eyes of Mine, which have seen Thy glory, the hideous sight of sin.

He arises and returns to the sleeping disciples, as if to escape from this unbearable sight of sin.

Once more He goes to the place of sorrow; and again sin is before His eyes. He seems unable to escape it. If He looks back into the past, He sees everywhere sin and abomination; and when He turns His eyes to the future, there again He gazes upon naught but sin and abomination. He sees the persecutions and trials of His Church, the infidelity and ingratitude of mankind whom He had come to save, the heresies and schisms, the desecration of His altars, the persecution of the priesthood instituted by Him. And alas, He sees also the blemished lives of some of His appointed servants; and, O my soul, He sees, too, my sins and my malice. Can it be possible that the pure Son of God must bear the guilt of all this wickedness? Shall all mankind be guiltless, and He carry the burden alone? His human nature, especially His Heart, rebels against this seemingly unjust demand of His heavenly Father. It is true that Jesus has set no limits to His sacrifice and that His spirit is willing; but the flesh is weak.

In this terrible trial He again feels the need of seeking solace, but once more finds His disciples asleep.

For the third time the sight of sin overwhelms Him. A frightful scene of the future is before Him: an immeasurable, endless line of blasphemies, desecrators, murderers, suicides, the unchaste, rioters, unworthy priests and religious, and an immense number of indifferent people who obstinately walk the broad road to destruction. Even those who have been highly favored by Him, the faithful and beloved of His Heart, remain cold and indifferent. Is it possible that He must die for these ungrateful ones? "Father, if it be possible, let this chalice pass from Me."

But during this vehement agitation and inexpressible loathing of His Heart, the Saviour of mankind recalls that the honor of His heavenly Father is at stake. He sees also the number of those who fear and love God; He sees also those who are of good will and who raise hearts and hands to the Heart of their Saviour to obtain strength in their weakness. And behold, the victorious love of His Heart reveals itself; it forces His blood through the pores of His sacred Body, while He prays with resignation to the Father: "My Father, if this chalice may not pass away, but I must drink it, Thy will be done" (Matt. 26:42).

Christian soul, contemplate this fearful agony of the Saviour's divine Heart. Have compassion for Him. Comfort Him in His desolation. Comfort Him, at least you, His friends. Indeed, this is the main object of the devotion to the Sacred Heart. And if God should require of you some great sacrifice, or should He send you a heavy cross, do not be disheartened; gaze upon the Heart of Jesus and say: "Heart of Jesus, bruised for our offenses, have mercy on us, and give strength to my heart, that I may avoid and detest sin above all things."

BEFORE HOLY COMMUNION

Holy Communion on the First Friday should always be a welcome opportunity to practice the virtue of compassion for the suffering Saviour. Therefore, try to remember the saddened Heart of your divine Friend; picture to yourself His passion and death on the cross. Meditate on the terrible pain which filled His Heart when Judas betrayed Him, when the rabble insulted Him, when most of His disciples forsook Him.

Faith

Most loving Jesus, really and substantially present in the Blessed Sacrament, I firmly believe that here Thou dost render full satisfaction for the sins of men, as Thou didst in the Garden of Olives, and that here, too, Thou dost say to Thy heavenly Father: "Not as I will, but as Thou wilt." I believe that the ingratitude of men, and especially my own coldness and indifference, intensified the agony within Thy Heart and caused the shedding of Thy precious Blood. And at this moment, here in the tabernacle, this same Heart beats for love of me, willing to offer Itself again for my salvation. Who would consider this possible, O Lord, if Thou Thyself hadst not revealed it: "Take ye, and eat: this is My Body, which shall be delivered for you" (Cor. 1:24). There can be no doubt. This is the same Body with the same Heart which once was sorrowful unto death because of my sins. It is Thy living Body, and hence also Thy most pure and compassionate Soul, which suffered so terribly to atone for my sins. Is it possible, O Lord, that Thou desirest to give Thy Heart, Thy Body and Thy Soul to me, notwithstanding my unworthiness and hardness of heart? Oh, increase my faith in Thy love for me, so that I may at least in the future atone for my sins and manifest my gratitude for all that Thou hast done and suffered for me.

Hope

O most Beloved of my soul, who didst undergo anguish and sorrow for my sake, it is from Thee alone that I hope for consolation and peace of conscience. In excruciating pain, and sorrowing for the blindness of mankind, Thou didst die on the cross; but Thou didst also speak the words of comfort: "I will see you again, and your heart shall rejoice; and your joy no man shall take from you" (John 16:22). And Thou didst add: "Amen, amen, I say to you: if you ask the Father anything in My name, He will give it to you" (John 16:23). Today I ask the Father who is in heaven, in Thy holy name, for the grace to realize my sinfulness ever more and more, to detest my sins and to do penance for the offenses which I have committed against Thy Sacred Heart. Through the infinite satisfaction which Thou didst make by Thy agony in the Garden and Thy death on the cross, I confidently hope to obtain forgiveness of my sins and eternal salvation.

Love and Contrition

Thou God of all consolation, Thou fountain of all joys and blessedness, Thou delight and bliss of the saints and angels, I contemplate with profound commiseration Thy humiliation in the mystery of Thy presence in the Blessed Sacrament. I hear Thee call to me: "Watch ye, and pray that ye enter not into temptation" (Matt. 26:41). How few there are who hear this call! Even among the faithful there are those who sleep in Thy very presence, like the three disciples in the Garden of Olives, while Thou sufferest alone, unheeded and misunderstood. Thou art truly a Man of sorrows! What a terrible weight upon Thy Heart are my sins and those of all mankind! Oh, that men would recognize the shame of sin and cease to heap ignominy upon Thee! Oh, that I, at least, would begin to love Thee with all my heart! This do I desire, O Jesus; I wish to receive Thee in order to watch and suffer with Thee. In the spirit of reparation and penance I offer Thee all my past sufferings. In the spirit of contrition, I offer Thee all my future trials. Do unto me according to Thy holy will.

Come now, O Beloved of my soul, come and enkindle in my heart the fire of Thy love. Unite my heart with Thine, so that with Thy help and following Thy example I may detest and abhor sin and forever love and honor God the Father in heaven.

Mary, my sorrowful Mother, all ye angels and saints, come to my aid from your thrones in heaven, that I may receive this Holy Communion worthily, and that it may be to me, as well as to the poor souls in purgatory and to sinners on earth, a pledge of eternal life.

"Divine Heart of Jesus, convert sinners, save the dying, set free the holy souls in purgatory." (Indulgence: 300 days.)

AFTER HOLY COMMUNION

Now the most propitious moment for the regulation of your spiritual affairs has arrived. Now, if ever, this prophecy of the Lord applies: "Promulgate, and have it promulgated, that I shall recognize no bounds in the granting of My graces to those who seek them in My heart." Therefore, use well the time allotted you for thanksgiving. Your eternity, perhaps, may depend upon these fifteen minutes.

Thanksgiving

My dearest Jesus, with all my heart I thank Thee for this unmerited grace, Thy visit to me. I welcome Thee with the greeting of the angels: Holy, holy, holy Lord, God of Hosts, heaven and earth are full of Thy glory. My soul trembles in ecstasy and my heart is inflamed with the fire of Thy love, because Thou hast come to me, Thou who didst love me unto death, yes, unto the death on the cross. Now I can sing with Thy spouse in the Canticle of Canticles: "I found Him whom my soul loveth. … and I will not let Him go" (3:4). No, nothing shall ever separate me from Thee again; neither my former faults and sins, because Thou hast generously forgiven them; nor this world with its false pomp; neither riches nor honors, pleasures nor sorrows, and certainly not death. Oh, give me today the consoling pledge that I shall die in Thy love. Amen.

Petitions to Jesus, Source of All Love

I embrace Thee with all my love, O sweetest Jesus, and will never permit Thee to leave me again; even Thy blessing is not sufficient for me if I cannot have Thee also as my greatest treasure and hope. O Thou vivifying Love of my soul, grant me a new life of grace and repair in me whatever has caused me to become indifferent or cold in my love of God. My God of love, who hast created me, let me be born again in Thy holy love. O my Love, who hast redeemed me, restore and redeem for Thyself all that I have neglected in the practice of my love for Thee. O God of Love, who didst redeem me through the Blood of Jesus Christ, sanctify me in Thy truth. O God of Love, who didst adopt me as Thy child, nourish and strengthen me according to Thy own Heart. O Love, who didst choose me for Thyself, help me to be Thine forever. O God of Love, who didst love me, though I am unworthy, give me the grace always to love Thee with all my heart, with all my soul and with all my strength. O God, Thou almighty Love, strengthen me in Thy love. O God, Thou most precious Love, help me to live only for Thee. O God, Thou most faithful Love, comfort me and come to my aid in every trial. O God, Thou victorious Love, help me to persevere unto the end. O Thou most fervent Love, who didst never forsake me, I recommend my soul into Thy hands. Receive me into Thy hands when I die; call me with Thine own lips and say: "Today thou shalt be with Me in Paradise; depart from thy place of exile and enter into the dawn of unchangeable eternity; there thou shalt verily see Me, the true Saviour, the beginning and end of all creatures. There thou shalt no longer experience any change, but shalt always be with Me. Even as I live, so thou, too, shalt live without end in blessed happiness with Me, thy God, thy Saviour and thy Love." All the powers, all the senses and emotions of my body and my soul say: Amen.

Petition

Benevolent Saviour, because my unworthiness has neither deterred Thee from renewing for me the mystery of Thy Flesh and Blood, nor prevented Thee from coming to my assistance, I am overwhelmed with so deep a trust in Thee that I dare to

confess my needs and my trials. Alas, my soul is so miserable
and weak! I desire most earnestly to serve Thee, but my
perverted will draws me to the service of the world; I desire to
please Thee, but my pride seeks the praise of creatures. I wish
to find my joy and my rest in Thee alone, but my heart seeks rest
and pleasure in the enjoyment of perishable things of this world.
I desire to love Thee, but besides Thee I love so many worldly
things which are not worthy of love. When, oh, when shall I
ever begin to love Thee above all things? At this moment my
heart is greatly inflamed by the fire of Thy love. Now I enjoy a
taste of Thy peace which the world cannot give. O Jesus, never
leave my heart again. Be Thou my Lord and King. O Thou
King of eternity, enchain me to Thee, lead me with a strong hand
on the way to perfection; draw me after Thee that I may at last
arrive safely in the land of comfort and peace, Thy heavenly
Kingdom. Amen.

*Prayer for the Conversion of the World Through the Divine
Heart of Jesus*

Eternal Father, I come to Thee through the Heart of Jesus,
who is our life, our truth and our way. Through this adorable
Heart, I adore Thee for all those who do not adore Thee; through
this Heart I love Thee for all those who do not love Thee; and I
believe in Thee for all those who, through willful blindness,
refuse to believe in Thee. In spirit I wander over the whole
world to seek souls which have all been redeemed by the
precious Blood of Jesus Christ. I embrace them all, in order to
offer them to Thee through the Sacred Heart of Jesus. Deign
Thou, through the Sacred Heart, to accept atonement for them
and my most humble prayers for their conversion. How canst
Thou, eternal Father, allow them not to know and serve Jesus,
who died for them? Thou seest, O divine Father, that they have
not yet awakened to a spiritual life; cause them to live the life of
faith through the Heart of Thy divine Son. Through this most
Sacred Heart I also recommend to Thee all Thy servants who
labor for the propagation of Thy Kingdom. In the name of Jesus
I beg of Thee that Thou mayest fill them with Thine holy spirit,
and that they may ever be under the guidance and protection of
the most Sacred Heart. O Jesus, Thou knowest all things that I
desire to beg of Thy Father; I beg them of Him through Thee,

because Thou art in the Father and the Father is in Thee. Do Thou with Him accomplish the conversion of sinners. Make them one with Thee here and in eternity. Amen.

"My Jesus, mercy." (Indulgence: 300 days. Plenary once a month if said every day.)

"Sweet Heart of Mary, be my salvation." (Indulgence: 300 days. Plenary once a month.)

"Omnipotence of the Father, help my frailty and rescue me from the depths of misery. Wisdom of the Son, direct all my thoughts, words and actions. Love of the Holy Spirit, be the source of all the operations of my soul, so that they may be entirely conformed to the divine will." (Indulgence: 500 days.)

FIRST FRIDAY IN APRIL

Heart of Jesus, pierced by a lance, have mercy on us.

"One of the soldiers with a spear opened His side, and immediately there came out blood and water." (John 19:34)

Meditation

The sufferings of the Sacred Heart are consummated. Having endured the ridicule of the high priests and the Pharisees, being exhausted from loss of blood and from the excruciating pains caused by the burning wounds on His hands and feet, the Heart of Jesus, which loved men so much, consumed Itself for their salvation. Broken is this Heart of the Child which had submitted Itself to the heavenly Father, and become obedient to Him unto death, yes, unto the death on the cross; broken is this Heart of the Saviour who so generously promised to refresh those who were burdened and heavily laden: "Come to Me, all you that labor, and are burdened, and I will refresh you" (Matt. 11:28).

Dear Christian, kneel down and adore this bleeding Heart of Jesus on the cross, and thank Him for the love which consumed Him like a burning fire throughout the thirty-three years of His life. Tarry a moment and await the events which are to come. Something sublime is about to occur. The prophecy of Zacharias is now to be fulfilled: "They shall look upon Me whom they have pierced" (Zach. 12:10).

It was the custom of old to use heavy clubs to break the bones of persons crucified, in order that, by hastening their death, the agony of these unfortunates might be shortened and their bodies receive speedier burial. Behold, the soldiers are breaking the bones of the two thieves who where crucified with Jesus. Now they approach the cross of Christ and see that He has expired. Therefore they do not break His bones; but one of the soldiers pierces the breast of the Saviour, thus opening His Heart, "and immediately there came out blood and water" (John 19:34). Astounded at this sight, St. John the Evangelist was impelled to profess solemnly that he saw with his own eyes the Heart of Jesus pierced with a spear. Why did John mention this incident? No doubt, it was because this beloved disciple foresaw the symbolic meaning of this act; he and the sorrowful Mother and Mary Magdalen were the first to call upon the Sacred Heart of Jesus with the petition: "Heart of Jesus, pierced with a lance, have mercy on us."

Indeed, after the Heart of Jesus had consummated the sacrifice for our salvation and had gained the victory over sin, It permitted Itself to be opened with a spear, in order to shed every drop of Its blood for us and give a visible proof of Its complete self-renunciation. In Jesus were thus fulfilled the prophetic words: "They shall look upon Me whom they have pierced" (Zach. 12:10).

How many afflicted souls have looked upon the pierced Heart of Jesus since St. John first beheld this tragic sight; how many have tasted of this inexhaustible fountain from which flow the necessary graces for eternal life! In this wound of the Sacred Heart St. Augustine sees the sacraments of the Church, without which the supernatural life of the soul is impossible. It is undoubtedly true that the entire life of grace in the Church and in individual souls had its beginning at the cross of Christ. What an infinite stream of graces flows from this pierced Heart to refresh and strengthen the hearts and souls of men! It floods the earth with its blessings; it reaches into the confines of purgatory and, rising in victory to the heavens, draws all to the glory of the Father.

Christian soul, look upon this pierced Heart of the Son of God and draw all grace from this fountain of life and sanctity. Wash your soul in His blood and strengthen it at the fountain of the sacraments. When you receive absolution in the sacrament of Penance, or assist at the Holy Sacrifice of the Mass, especially when you receive the Saviour into your heart in Holy Communion, remember that these graces came to you through the Sacred Heart of Jesus; look up to that Heart in gratitude, for It was pierced with a lance because of your sins.

DEVOTION FOR COMMUNION

Always receive Holy Communion as if it were for the first and last time in your life and as if your eternal happiness depended upon it alone. Holy Communion should never lose the charm of novelty, even if we receive daily, because day after day it is a new miracle of the love of the Son of God for sinners.

BEFORE HOLY COMMUNION

O most loving Lord, Jesus Christ, Thou giver of all consolation and wonderful spectacle for angels and men! O divine Vase filled with blessings and graces, Lord and King! Thou didst permit Thy holy side to be opened with a lance. I beg Thee to open unto me this portal of Thy infinite mercy; permit me to enter through Thy opened side into the mysterious citadel of Thy most loving Heart. Make my heart one with Thine in inseparable love; inflame it with deepest love for Thee that Thou mayest live in me and I in Thee, and that we may remain united for all eternity. May the lance of Thy love penetrate deeply my indifferent heart and all the powers of my soul; may no other love ever take possession of me, so that henceforth I shall seek consolation and joy in Thee alone. May my heart be open to Thee only; may it be ever closed to the world and to Satan, and may it always and everywhere be protected against the onslaughts of sin by the sign of Thy holy cross. Amen.

Faith, Hope, Love and Contrition
O Jesus, the open wound of Thy Sacred Heart constrains me to come to Thee. I hear again Thy tender voice extending Thy invitation to sinners: "Come to me, all you that labor, and are burdened, and I will refresh you." I firmly believe that it was not a mere chance which drove the lance of the soldier into Thy Heart. No; Thy love, which rested not even in death, permitted the opening of Thy Heart in order to provide for me an entrance into this Thy sanctuary. I lay my hand into the wound of Thy side, and, like St. Thomas, find strength of faith in Thy love for me. My Lord and my God, hear the humble profession of faith. Yes, I believe in the love of Thy Heart; I also believe that Thy Heart is open to me in the Blessed Sacrament, and that it permits my entrance therein through Holy Communion.

"O Lord, increase in us the Faith." (Indulgence: 500 days each time. Plenary once a month.)

Full of confidence I approach the open wound from which flowed blood and water for the atonement of my sins and the strengthening of my soul. O sweetest Saviour, permit me to rest in the sacred wound of Thy side. There I shall be fortified against the assaults of Satan and the temptations of the flesh; there I shall find alleviation in suffering, and consolation in loneliness and sorrow.

Sweetest Jesus, night and day Thy Heart is open to me in the Blessed Sacrament of the Altar, eager to grant me all necessary graces. How often have I saddened that Heart by my indifference in the reception of Thy Flesh and Blood! How often have I forsaken Thee and followed my own evil desires! Would that I could say with St. Peter: "Lord, Thou knowest all things: Thou knowest that I love Thee" (John 21:17). Alas, my past life does not justify my speaking as St. Peter did. However, I promise Thee that from this day until my death I will love Thee with all my heart. I desire to repay love for love. Deign to permit one drop of Thy precious Blood, like refreshing dew, to enter my soul, so that it may be filled with the incense of Thy sweetness and goodness, and that it may wish for nothing more that to love Thee and be loved by Thee.

"Sweet Heart of my Jesus, make me love Thee ever more and more!" (Indulgence: 300 days. Plenary once a month.)

Prayer to the Sorrowful Mother of God
Mary, Mother of Jesus and my mother, when thou didst present thy divine Son in the temple at Jerusalem, thou didst hear the solemn prophecy of Simeon: "Thy own soul a sword shall pierce, that out of many hearts, thoughts may be revealed" (Luke 2:35). It is with deepest shame that I confess having caused thee this pain, for I also am guilty of grieving the divine Heart of thy Son. Oh, do not judge me too severely. Harken to the voice of thy Son: "Woman, behold thy son" (John 19:26). May it please thee to be a kind mother to me, and to obtain for me from the Heart of Jesus the mercies and graces which I so sorely need, especially that I may receive my Saviour worthily today and also when He comes as Viaticum at the hour of death.

AFTER HOLY COMMUNION

When you receive Holy Communion worthily, Jesus meets you in a loving embrace. Greet Him in the words of St. Paul:

"Lord, what wilt Thou have me to do?" (Acts 9:6) And Jesus in return greets you: "What will ye that I do to you?" (Matt. 20:32)

Listen to the voice of Jesus: "Behold, my child," He says, "I live now in you and you in Me. Contemplate the wounds in My hands and feet, turn your ear to the wound in My side and listen to what I have to say to you: My child, what have I done to you? Have I displeased you? Speak, speak at least now, while I am with you. I have delivered you out of the land of Egypt, and you have nailed Me, your Redeemer, to the cross. Once in the sacrament of Baptism, and later so often in the sacrament of Penance, I have delivered you from the slavery of Satan, and you have repeatedly fashioned a cross for Me. With an eternal love have I loved you, and you have pierced My Heart with a lance. But do not lose courage; even this last wound shall be a pledge of My love for you. I have written your name deeply into My Heart and into the wounds of My hands and feet. I ask only your love in return. If I request a sacrifice of you today or at some future time, then remember the wound in My side; if an earthly love or some worldly advantage tempts you to leave Me, then, too, remember the wound in My heart in which your name is written, and resolve to belong only to Me."

Most loving Saviour, I cannot find words to thank Thee as Thou deservest for this new manifestation of Thy love. I can only declare that I love Thee now and henceforth shall always love Thee. I desire to atone for my past lukewarmness by grateful submission to Thy sweet yoke. Never again will I withdraw my allegiance to Thee; let me find refuge in Thy Heart against the snares of Satan, the allurements of the world and the pride of life. May the memory of my past sins keep me humble, and may Thy goodness and mercy strengthen me in time of temptation. O Jesus, meek and humble of Heart, make my heart like unto Thine. Heart of Jesus, pierced with a lance, wound my heart with Thy love.

Three Petitions to the Divine Heart of Jesus

O Jesus, inexhaustible fountain of love, from the innermost depths of Thy Heart Thou didst call from the cross: "I thirst." Thou didst thirst for the salvation of mankind. I implore Thee, inflame all the impulses of our hearts, that they may strive only after virtue; do Thou quench completely in us all sensual appetite and all desire for worldly things. Amen.

O Jesus, Thou sweetness of all hearts, Thou only delight of souls, through the bitterness of the vinegar and gall which Thou didst taste, grant us the grace at the hour of our death worthily to receive Thy Flesh and Blood for the salvation and comfort of our souls. Amen.

O Jesus, Almighty King, delight of mankind, remember the fear and pain which Thy Heart endured because of the agony of death and the malice of the Jews; Thou didst feel deserted by the Father and didst call with a loud voice: "My God, My God, why hast Thou forsaken Me?" I beseech Thee, O Lord, our God, that through this agony of Thy Heart Thou mayest not forsake us in our needs. Amen.

Consecration

O adorable Heart of Jesus, is it not my duty to comfort Thee in Thy loneliness, knowing that Thou dost remain in our midst in this Sacrament of love in order to sweeten our exile here on earth? Thou dost give me Thy Heart. Shall I not give Thee mine?

Giving myself to Thee, O Lord, is my greatest gain; for in doing so I find the inexhaustible treasure of a Heart, a Heart which loves, a Heart unselfish and loyal as I desire my own to be. Though I offer Thee nothing, I constantly receive favors from Thee. I cannot vie with Thee in generosity, yet I deeply love Thee. Deign to accept my poor heart, though it be worthless; but, if loved by Thee, it will become precious by Thy grace.

Heart of Jesus in the Blessed Sacrament, I consecrate to Thee all the faculties of my soul and all the strength of my body. I will make every effort to know Thee better, to love Thee more ardently and to teach others to know and love Thee. I desire to labor only for Thy honor and to do the will of Thy heavenly Father. Here in Thy presence I consecrate every moment of my life to adoration and thanksgiving for this incomparable gift, in reparation for my cruel indifference and as a perpetual atonement; may the prayers which I offer Thee become fruitful by Thy grace, and through Thee ascend to the throne of mercy for the eternal glory of God. Amen.

FIRST FRIDAY IN MAY

Heart of Jesus, our life and resurrection, have mercy on us.

"I am the resurrection and the life." (John 11:25)

Meditation

A short distance from Jerusalem was the small village of Bethany, the home of the penitent Mary Magdalen, who resided there with her brother Lazarus and her sister Martha. From the day that Mary had received the grace of conversion, she had renounced her life of sin and had surrendered herself to the divine Saviour in sincere love and piety. Jesus loved to visit her home. These three simple but noble-minded people always received Jesus most kindly and loved Him dearly. Jesus called Lazarus His friend.

Jesus had reached the last days of His earthly life. The high-priests and Pharisees persecuted Him relentlessly. With His disciples He had retired beyond the Jordan, when Lazarus, after a short illness, died. Jesus, the Omniscient, was aware of it. His Heart was sorely tried by the loss of His friend, but He was not despondent. His divine Heart, which loved Lazarus so much, constrained Him to work one of His greatest miracles. He told His disciples that Lazarus was sleeping, but that He would go to awaken him.

Informed of His master coming, Martha hastened to meet the Master, greeting Him with the words: "Lord, if Thou hast been here, my brother had not died" (John 11:21). But she did not lose hope. Remembering the love of the Heart of Jesus, she added: "But now also I know that whatsoever Thou wilt ask of God, God will give it Thee" (John 11:22). Jesus said to her: "Thy brother shall rise again." Then Jesus revealed to Martha a great mystery of His Sacred Heart, saying: "I am the resurrection and the life: he that believeth in Me, although he be dead, shall live."

Jesus approached the grave. Unspeakable pain pierced His Heart when He beheld Mary and the group of mourning friends; He, too, wept. They whispered to one another: "Behold how He loved him." Jesus then commanded the stone be removed from the grave. Fully conscious that the heavenly Father had given

Him divine power, the Worker of miracles called with a loud voice: "Lazarus, come forth!" And he who had been buried four days came forth from the grave alive.

What miraculous power was manifested here by the Sacred Heart! Fall on your knees, O Christian, and pray with the full conviction of your faith: "Heart of Jesus, our life and resurrection, have mercy on us." What Jesus did in behalf of Lazarus He wishes to do also for you. He desires to awaken you to a new life. He does not desire the death of the sinner but that he be converted and live. The sight of your soul, impoverished, distressed, and perhaps even wounded mortally by the sting of grievous sin, arouses the compassion of His Heart and moves him to tears. Did He not come that all may have life, and my have it abundantly? Did He not merit the life of grace for all mankind by His obedience, His sufferings and His death? Did He not conquer death by His glorious resurrection? Take courage, therefore. Have confidence in the Heart of Jesus, and believe in the power of His love. "For God so loved the world, as to give His only-begotten Son: that whoever believeth in Him, may not perish, but may have life everlasting" (John 3:16). "I am the resurrection and the life" (John 11:25). Make a contrite and humble confession of your sins; then, when you receive Holy Communion, you will be assured by the words of the priest: "May the Body of our Lord Jesus Christ keep thy soul unto life everlasting." Then this Holy Communion will be a pledge to you of a glorious resurrection on the last day because our divine Saviour has said: "He that eateth My Flesh, and drinketh My Blood, hath everlasting life: and I will raise him up in the last day" (John 6:55).

Everything depends on our last end. All is well that ends well! We sinful human beings must always remember the four last things in fear and trembling. Shall I be saved? On the day of the resurrection the trumpet will sound, the earth will tremble, graves will open, and the voice of the Son of God will be heard; then, when my soul will be reunited with my body, which has been the cause of so many of my sins, what will be my feelings? Will I fear and tremble or will joy fill my soul? This is indeed an earnest thought, which may rightly fill even the mighty with fear and terror. But take heart, Christian soul. If you truly love the Sacred Heart and firmly resolve, in spite of your frequent falls, to seek refuge in this Heart, it is impossible for you to fail in the purpose for which you were created and for which the Heart of Jesus suffered so much. Jesus does not want us to be in doubt about His mercy and generosity toward us. His words cannot be misunderstood: "I am the resurrection and the life: he that believeth in Me, although he be dead, shall live" (John 11:25).

DEVOTION FOR COMMUNION

Before going to the Table of the Lord, examine yourself again to see whether there is still some slight affection for sin hidden in your heart. Should you discover such a fault, humbly confess it to your Saviour in Holy Communion, and beg of Him the grace to conquer it completely.

BEFORE HOLY COMMUNION

Confidence
Dearest Lord and Master, adorable Saviour, how anxiously did Martha and Mary long for Thy arrival when their beloved brother lay sick unto death, and Thou, their dearest Friend and most able Physician, wast far away. Behold, today another petitioner calls upon Thee, who feels a still greater need of Thy remedies, because he suffers more from ailment of the soul than of the body. Alas, it is my own fault that hitherto I have not accepted Thy remedy. Thou wast always so near and hast often called to me from Thy tabernacle: "Come to me, all you that labor and are burdened, and I will refresh you" (Matt. 11:28). Yes, if I had come, my soul would not have died. "But now also I know that whatsoever Thou wilt ask of God, God will give it Thee" (John 11:22). I, too, believe firmly that I shall rise again through the grace which flows from Thy Heart. Therefore, I hasten to Thee this day, fall at Thy feet and confidently pray: "O Lord, say but the word, and my soul shall be healed." Oh come, oh come, Emmanuel, awaken my soul from its sleep of spiritual sloth, and arouse it to a new life of virtue. Amen.

"Sacred Heart of Jesus, I trust in Thee." (Indulgence: 300 days. Plenary once a month.)

Faith

"The blind see, the lame walk, the lepers are cleansed, the deaf hear, the dead rise again" (Matt. 11:5). No greater proof of Thy divinity, O Jesus, is required that this. I believe, O Lord, that Thou art Christ, the Son of the living God, who didst come into this world, and that Thou art present among us day and night. One day Thou didst speak with power and majesty to the dead young man of Naim: "Young man, I say to thee, arise!" and to Thy friend Lazarus who had been in the grave four days: "Lazarus, come forth!" How could I ever doubt those words which Thou didst speak to Thy disciples at the Last Supper: "Take ye and eat. This is My Body … Drink ye all of this. For this is My Blood" (Matt. 26:26-28). And how could I doubt the life-giving power of Thy Flesh and Blood, remembering Thy solemn promise: "He that eateth My Flesh, and drinketh My Blood, hath everlasting life: and I will raise him up in the last day" (John 6:55). With a firm and unswerving faith, I believe and profess that Thou art the resurrection and the life. He that believeth in Thee shall live, although he be dead.

Humility and Contrition

Who am I, that I dare approach the divine Worker of miracles, the Master of life and death, and invite Him to enter my soul? Am I not the one who has so often neglected Him, so often carelessly passed His sanctuary without heeding His invitation? Must I not confess that I am the one who through my fault, through my greatest fault, have so often offended Him? At last, O Lord, I am enlightened; I acknowledge my unbounded folly, my misery, my weakness and my distress. Deign to accept the sorrow of my soul as proof of my willingness to return to Thee, and to be converted by Thee to a more perfect life. Remove from my soul the heavy weight laid upon it by the knowledge of my sinfulness; loose the bonds which still chain me to my sinful past. Call with a loud voice, O Lord, and let Thy divine words ring in my soul: "Flee from the grave of sinful habits and spiritual indolence! Come forth into the light of grace! Arise! Have courage, and eat of the Bread of life. Fortify yourself, because you may still have a long pilgrimage before you."

"Eucharistic Heart of Jesus, have mercy on us." (Indulgence:

300 days.)

Three Prayers to Our Heavenly Mother

O purest Virgin Mary, through thy immaculate purity thou didst prepare a most pleasing dwelling-place in thy womb for the Son of God. I beg of thee to intercede for me that I may be cleansed from all stains of sin.

O most humble Virgin Mary, by thy deep humility thou didst merit to be raised in dignity above all the angels and saints. Obtain for me through thy merits that all my sins of omission may be forgiven.

O loving Virgin Mary, through the boundless love which preserved thee in closest union with God, I beg of thee to obtain for me the grace to receive Jesus worthily in the Holy Eucharist and to find in Him my greatest happiness. Amen.

AFTER HOLY COMMUNION

Thanksgiving

I thank Thee, my Redeemer, with all my heart, for the honor of Thy visit and for the treasures of grace which Thou, out of the fullness of Thy Heart, dost grant to all those who take refuge in Thee. Thou givest me life, for Thou art indeed the resurrection and the life. With thee, O Jesus, joy, courage and a new life have once more entered my soul. Now I can say with the Apostle: "I live, now not I, but Christ liveth in me" (Gal. 2:20).

My dearest Saviour, live always in me, and help me with Thy grace even after Thou art no longer substantially present in my body. Nothing shall ever separate me from Thee again; neither trials, nor sufferings nor death, nor even the false pomp of the world. Oh no, my Jesus; Thy love is mightier than death itself. Oh, give me a deep love for Thee, and grant me the strength to die rather than ever to sin again.

"Sweet Heart of my Jesus, make me love Thee ever more and more." (Indulgence: 300 days. Plenary once a month.)

Love

O divine Heart of my Saviour, who art all goodness and perfection, I desire to love Thee as intimately as Thou deservest to be loved. Cleanse my soul from whatever may be displeasing to Thee; inflame it with Thy divine love, that I may desire and strive after nothing but Thee, my God and my all. Henceforth, at least, I will love Thee with all my heart, consecrate to Thee every moment of my life, and thus endeavor to atone for my past negligence. I envy those happy souls who have consecrated themselves to Thy service from their earliest youth. How is it possible, O Eternal Beauty, that I could deny and offend Thee, the most gracious of all beings? How sorry I am, ever to have offended Thee! Should I ever again be in danger of committing sin, I beg Thee to let me die in Thy love rather than fall in my weakness; because to live without loving Thee is more painful than death. God, my greatest good, I long for the happy moment when Thou shalt forever be mine in heaven. There I shall know Thee and see Thee face to face. In heaven I shall love Thee from the bottom of my heart and with all the strength of my soul, and shall praise and glorify Thy infinite mercy forever and ever. Amen.

Prayer for the Conversion of Sinners

O my Lord and Saviour, Jesus Christ, not for my soul alone do I beg the blessings which flow from Thy Sacred Heart, but I pray also for the welfare of all poor sinners, for whom Thou didst suffer and die. Urge them all to come to Thy Heart, O Lord, to this fountain, yes, this ocean, of Thy infinite love; that in Thy Heart they may be freed from their sins, and that henceforth they may accept Thee as their gracious Spouse. Grant to them all, and to me also, eternal life in Thy Heart. Amen.

Petition

Jesus, my life, my hope and my firm faith, Thou didst say: "Ask, and it shall be given you: seek, and you shall find: knock, and it shall be opened to you" (Matt. 7:7). With a childlike trust I have received Thee into my heart, and I know that Thou wilt hear my prayer. I beseech Thee to bestow Thy grace upon me, my parents and relatives, my friends and benefactors, upon all those for whom I have promised to pray, as well as upon those for whom I am in duty bound to pray, that they may obtain temporal and eternal happiness. Grant that hereafter we may meet again in Thy love and in the contemplation of Thy glorified Heart. Thou art the resurrection and the life; oh, grant the life of Thy grace in plentiful abundance to all who are near and dear to me. Remember especially those who are careless in the fulfillment of their duties.

Do thou, O Mother of divine grace, confirm my prayer before the throne of the Lamb; and you angels and saints, especially you patron saints of my relatives and friends, help us to pray, praise and glorify God. Help us to love Him, who is the Way, the Truth and the Life. Amen.

Prayer to Our Lady of the Sacred Heart
Remember, Our Lady of the Sacred Heart, the ineffable power which thy divine Son has given Thee over His adorable Heart. Full of confidence in thy merits, we now implore thy protection. O heavenly treasure of the Heart of Jesus, of that Heart which is the inexhaustible source of all graces, and which thou mayest open when thou pleasest, in order to distribute among men all the treasures of love and mercy, of light and salvation, which it contains, grant us, we beseech thee, the favors we solicit ... No, we cannot meet with a refusal, and since thou art our Mother, Our Lady of the Sacred Heart, favorably hear and grant our prayers. Amen.

"Our Lady of the Sacred Heart, pray for us." (Indulgence: 300 days.)

"Most holy and immaculate Virgin Mary, Mother of God and our Mother, speak on our behalf to the Heart of Jesus, who is thy Son and our Brother."

FIRST FRIDAY IN JUNE

Heart of Jesus, burning furnace of charity, have mercy on us.

"Having loved His own who were in the world, He loved them unto the end." (John 13:1)

Meditation

The life of Jesus on earth was an unbroken act of love. Learned theologians state that from the first moment of the Incarnation Jesus had full knowledge of His future life; and they say that at His birth He greeted His heavenly Father with the prophetic words of the Psalmist: "Sacrifice and oblation Thou didst not desire … then said I, Behold I come" (Ps. 39:7-8).

In the very beginning of His earthly life Jesus offered His Heart to the heavenly Father as a most pleasing sacrifice. Like the bush of the Old Testament, which burned but was not consumed, the Heart of Jesus is aflame with unending love for God and man. Yes! His Heart is a burning furnace of love. For thirty years He concealed the flames of His love from the public eye; only Mary and Joseph were silent witnesses of it. But at last He could control it no longer. He passed through all parts of Palestine proclaiming by word and deed: "I am come to cast fire on the earth: and what will I, but that it be kindled" (Luke 12:49). Until then it had been cold upon the earth. A winter of thousands of years lay on the hearts of men. But now, at last, the sun of the Heart of Jesus rose to give light and warmth, and the spring of life filled the land. A new joy came into the hearts of men: "The blind see, the lame walk, the lepers are made clean, the deaf hear, the dead rise again, to the poor the Gospel is preached" (Luke 7:22). Blessed are the poor in spirit, for theirs is the kingdom of God; and blessed are all those who are not scandalized by the Sun of Love, but warm their hearts in Its rays. The entire public life of Jesus as told by the Evangelists, is like a magnet, drawing all men to Christ.

Alas, this springtime of the love of the Sacred Heart lasted only three years. Summer must follow the spring, and the Sun of Love must reach Its zenith on the cross, so that It may enlighten and animate the whole world. Jesus Himself said that once He was lifted up, He would draw all hearts to His own.

Jesus loved His disciples and Apostles with a particular love. The thought that soon He must be separated from them rested heavily on His Heart. Those whom He had loved, He loved unto the end. At the Last Supper He fulfilled the promise which He had made to the Apostles, and carried out a divine plan which emanated from His loving Heart. He took bread, blessed it, broke it and gave it to His Apostles saying: "Take ye, and eat, this is My Body." And taking the chalice, He gave thanks, and gave to them, saying: "Drink ye all of this. For this is My Blood" (Matt. 26: 26-28). In St. Luke we read how Jesus desired them to continue this solemn act in the Church: "Do this for a commemoration of Me" (Luke 22: 19). Through these words Jesus gave power to the Apostles and their successors for all time, to change bread and wine into His own Flesh and Blood. On that most solemn occasion the Apostles remembered the prophetic words of Jesus, which had been displeasing to many of His disciples: "He that eateth My Flesh, and drinketh My Blood, abideth in Me, and I in him" (John 6:57).

This sacrament of love was to remain with us, even after Jesus had offered His Heart as a sacrifice on the tree of the cross, and then departed from this earth. For He had given to the Apostles and their successors, the bishops and priests, the power to preserve to the world the same Flesh, the same Blood, the same Heart, substantially united with the Soul of Christ. His Heart yearned for this presence among men. It yearned to show Itself to be a burning furnace of love for all future generations, a sun to inflame the hearts of men. For this reason the most holy Sacrament of the Altar is rightly called the sacrament of His love, the sacrament of His Heart.

And yet this love of Jesus in the Blessed Sacrament is insulted and despised. A cold breath is wafted over the earth, benumbing hearts with indifference. How few there are who truly love their Creator and Redeemer! So many other warm themselves in the rays of the sun which God has place in the firmament, but with careless unconcern permit the Sun of His loving Heart in His Blessed Sacrament to shine and give warmth in loneliness. Even those who know this Son of Love and often visit the Saviour and receive Him in Holy Communion remain cold and indifferent.

Christian soul, you know how much the Heart of Jesus

endures on account of this isolation and, by His own words, you know, too, that the revelations which He made to St. Margaret Mary and the introduction of the devotion to the Sacred Heart were a last effort to draw men to Himself and to save souls. Oh, do you, at least, let your heart be inflamed with love for Jesus. Visit Him in the Blessed Sacrament, take Him into your heart, especially during this month and on the Feast of the Sacred Heart, and often pray: "Heart of Jesus, burning with love of us, inflame our hearts with love of Thee." (Indulgence: 300 days. Plenary once a month.)

DEVOTION FOR COMMUNION

Before each Holy Communion you must have an earnest desire to love Jesus, because love is the best preparation and is to be preferred to any form of prayer. Jesus, who looks into our hearts, does not desire words or forms of prayer if our hearts have no part in them: "If I speak with the tongues of men and of angels, and have not charity, I am become as sounding brass, or a tinkling cymbal" (1 Cor. 13:1).

BEFORE HOLY COMMUNION

O Heart of my Saviour, inflamed for love of me, is it indeed true that I am to be so fortunate as to receive Thee, and to shelter Thee within my heart? Am I to receive Thee, O Jesus, who art my God and Saviour? Thee, who hast created me and the whole world? Shall I be allowed to receive that most holy Flesh and Blood which has redeemed me? Thy Heart, Thy sweetest, most loving, divine Heart, which will open heaven to me? Oh, how happy I am to receive this wondrous gift. Even the angels in heaven may well envy me. Thou, O Lord, who sittest in glory upon Thy heavenly throne; Thou, the King of glory and bliss; Thou, whom all the angels humbly adore as their God and Master, Thou dost conceal, out of love for me, Thy glory under the humble appearances of this Sacrament of love. This Sacrament is not a picture nor a statue representing Thee, but Thy very Self. Remember, my soul, that Jesus truly comes to you. In a few moments you will have the happiness not only to kneel at His feet, as did Mary Magdalen, but to take into your very self His Sacred Heart.

Am I really worthy of such a magnificent gift? Am I not a miserable, poverty-stricken creature; a worm, that deserves to be trodden into the dust and be buried in the fires of hell? How shall I dare to receive Thee in my great unworthiness? It is only too true, my God and Saviour, that I am not worthy that Thou shouldst enter my heart; I am not worthy to receive Thy most pure and Sacred Heart into my own, since I am only a weak creature brought forth by Thee out of nothing, and Thou art the Son of the living God. But because I have been prepared by Thy grace, and because Thou, my sweetest Jesus, has so earnestly invited me, I will now approach in all humility to receive Thee.

O my dear Saviour, I have an insatiable longing to receive Thee, the true Paschal Lamb. I hunger and thirst after Thee. Thy flesh is meat indeed and Thy Blood is drink indeed. Whosoever eateth Thy Flesh and drinketh Thy Blood liveth in Thee and Thou in him. Oh, that I could give joy to the heavenly Father, who gave Thee wholly to me! Oh, that I could give to Thy Heart at least a little joy, and could atone to some extent, by my devotion and love, for all the insults which have been heaped upon this holy Sacrament since the time of its institution! And lastly, I wish most earnestly that I could honor and glorify Thee, O Holy Spirit, through whose mysterious power Jesus was conceived in the womb of the Blessed Virgin Mary! Would that I could today receive Thee, dearest Jesus, with the same love with which Thy purest Mother received Thee from the Holy Spirit! Would that I could receive Holy Communion like St. Aloysius, St. Francis Xavier, St. Catherine, or like the other great saints of the Church.

Come, then, and give joy to my heart, Thou divine, Thou loving and heavenly Heart of my God. Come, O Jesus, my life, my bliss, my God and my all. "As the deer panteth after the fountains of water, so my soul panteth after Thee, O God" (Ps. 41:1). O come, my Jesus, my love. Amen.

Prayer to the Sacred Heart of Jesus

"Behold, my most loving Jesus, to what an excess Thy boundless love has carried Thee. Of Thine own Flesh and Blood Thou hast made ready for me a divine banquet, in order to give me Thyself. What was it that impelled Thee to this transport of love? It was Thy Heart, Thy loving Heart. O adorable Heart of my Jesus, burning furnace of divine love; within Thy most sacred Wound receive Thou my soul; that in that school of charity I may learn to requite the love of that God who has given such wonderful proofs of His love. Amen." (Indulgence: 500 days. Plenary once a month.)

"Eucharistic Heart of Jesus, have mercy on us." (Indulgence: 300 days.)

AFTER HOLY COMMUNION

Jesus is in my heart. Let this thought dominate your soul for some time. Enjoy these moments to their fullest extent, in the knowledge that you possess Him whom heaven and earth cannot contain, and that you love Him who first loved you with an undoubted love, and who desires to love you unto the end, forever and ever.

Thanksgiving

My sweetest Saviour, words cannot express the heartfelt gratitude I owe Thee for the wonderful favor Thou didst grant me today. Thou in me – Thou, the Highest, Most Perfect and Most Lovable – in me, the lowliest, poorest and most despicable of Thy creatures. What impelled Thee to disregard the infinite chasm that exists between Thee and me, and to come to be my strength? I know, O Jesus; it was Thy love, that infinite love of Thy Sacred Heart. Praise and thanksgiving be to Thee for this favor.

I adore Thy most Sacred Heart, the burning furnace of love, the bush, burning, yet unconsumed, from which issue the voice of the eternal Father: "I am the Lord thy God; I have seen the misery of thy heart, and have resolved to liberate thee from the bondage of sin, and to grant thee the sweet freedom of the children of God. Oh, loose the shoes from my feet, keep thyself free from sinful inclinations, and consider with all reverence that the most Sacred Heart of My Son is now within thee."

O Heart of Jesus, burning furnace of love, in deepest reverence I adore Thee. Inflame my heart and cleanse it from all consequences of sin; enkindle within me an ardent desire to love Thee, and to possess nothing but Thee alone.

Alas, I have so little of that love. Make me rich, O Jesus, grant me the purest gold of Thy love. I am destitute of good works; grant me the grace to sanctify every moment of my life, in order to clothe my soul in the spotless garment of the children of God.

Oh, that I could ever become more confirmed to Thee, my sublime Ideal! Make me pure and modest, humble and meek of heart; implant into my heart a holy zeal for the honor and glory of Thy heavenly Father; grant me the grace to overcome my evil inclinations, and to renounce everything that might cloud the friendship between Thee and me.

"O Heart of love, I place all my trust in Thee: for though I fear all things from my weakness, I hope all things from Thy mercies." (Indulgence: 300 days. Plenary once a month.)

Indulgenced Prayer to the Eucharistic Heart of Jesus
O Eucharistic Heart, O sovereign Love of our Lord Jesus, who has instituted the august Sacrament, in order to dwell here on earth with us and to give to our souls Thy Flesh as food and Thy Blood as drink, we confidently trust, O Lord Jesus, in the supreme love which instituted the most Holy Eucharist. Here, in the presence of this Victim, it is just that we should adore, confess, and exalt this love, as the great storehouse of the life of Thy Church. This love is an earnest invitation for us, as though Thou didst say to us: "See how I love you, giving you My Flesh as food, and My Blood as drink; by this union I desire to excite your charity, I desire to unite you to Myself, I desire to effect the transformation of your souls into My crucified Self, I who am the Bread of Eternal Life.

"Give Me, then, your hearts, live in My life, and you shall live in God."

We recognize, O Lord, that such is the appeal of Thy Eucharistic Heart, and we thank Thee for it, and we desire earnestly to respond to it. Grant us the grace to be keenly alive to this supreme love, with which, before Thy Passion, Thou didst invite us to receive Thy Body as food. Print deeply on our souls the firm determination to respond faithfully to this invitation. Give us devotion and reverence whereby we may honor and receive worthily the gift of Thy supreme love, and of Thy Eucharistic Heart. Grant that we may thus be able, with

Thy grace, to celebrate profitably the remembrance of Thy Passion, to make reparation for our offenses and our coldness, to nourish and increase our love for Thee, and to keep ever living within our hearts this seed of a blessed immortality. Amen. (Indulgence: 5 years at Exposition.)

Reparation and Consecration

O divine Heart of Jesus, Thou didst love us poor mortals to the extent of giving Thyself as a Victim, sacrificing and exhausting Thyself, in order to manifest that love. Induced by this same love, Thou didst remain among us mortals in the most Holy Eucharist, daily offering Thyself as a Victim for our salvation, and becoming the Food of our souls. All this Thou didst in the past and dost still continue to do; and Thou wouldst even be still more generous toward us, if it were possible, in order to receive our love in return. Nevertheless, many hearts remain cold and indifferent, through their disrespect, indifference, insults and even unworthy Communions. Even those who are in a special manner consecrated to Thee often offend Thy loving Heart. We are deeply mortified to think that we, too, must be numbered among the ungrateful.

Behold, O Lord, with contrite hearts we kneel before Thee to make reparation in Thy own name, as well as in the name of all mankind, for the shameful manner in which we have neglected Thee. Have mercy on us and pardon our negligence. Cancel our debt to Thee in the Blood of Thy divine Heart, and remember no more our perfidy, but only Thy love and Thy mercy. Let the fullness of Thy blessing descend upon the entire Christian world, upon the Holy Father, upon our friends and relatives, and especially upon us who are assembled in Thy presence.

United in prayer before Thee, O most holy and divine Heart, we freely consecrate ourselves to Thee; our souls and bodies, our life and all our actions, all our trials and sufferings. Grant that in the future we may live only for Thy honor and glory, and that in eternity we may be entirely consumed by love for Thee. O Heart of Jesus, Thou only and sweet bliss of our souls, engrave our names so indelibly into Thy Heart, and imprint Thy love so deeply into our hearts, that we may never forget Thee, nor ever be separated from Thee. In Thy service we wish to live and die. Amen.

FIRST FRIDAY IN JULY

Heart of Jesus, patient and most merciful, have mercy on us.

"I am the good shepherd. The good shepherd giveth his life for his sheep." (John 10:11)

Meditation

There is nothing to which the heart of man is more sensitive than to insults, ridicule or cruel affronts. Christian soul, consider well that every sin is an insult to the Sacred Heart of Jesus, contempt for His love and Commandments and an affront to His loving benevolence toward His creatures. Then count, if you can, all the insults which have ever been heaped upon the Sacred Heart; consider, for example, the number of your own sins.

This loving Heart would certainly be justified were It to turn from man in disgust in order to give Its whole affection to Its heavenly Father.

But what does Jesus actually do? He is patient and most merciful toward those who offend Him. In the City of Sichem there lived a woman, an adulteress, who had caused the Sacred Heart unspeakable pain. Jesus rested near the city. He was tired, hungry and thirsty, and sat down to rest at the Well of Jacob, while the disciples entered the city to obtain food. Jesus waited … waited patiently; and behold, the woman approached to draw water from the well. Jesus spoke kindly to her, telling her of the water that leads to eternal life. He spoke to her conscience, revealing her sins; and thus became her Messiah, her Saviour.

On another occasion Jesus was the guest of Simon, the Pharisee. A woman entered the house, her tresses hanging loosely about her shoulders. With tears in her eyes she knelt at the feet of Jesus, washing them with her tears and drying them with her hair. She anointed His feet with balsam and kissed them repeatedly. Although Jesus knew that this woman had often offended Him during her sinful life, nevertheless, He permitted her to perform these acts upon His Person. Simon, the Pharisee, however, thought that if Jesus was indeed a prophet He must know of her sinfulness and therefore repulse her. How little does this Pharisee know the Heart of Jesus, which is so ready to pardon a truly contrite heart, and which even now speaks to this sinful adulteress, who had given so much scandal, these words of pardon: "Thy sins are forgiven thee … Thy faith hath made thee safe, go in peace" (Luke 7:48, 50).

With the same patience and mercy Jesus receives the prodigal son and invites the heavens to rejoice because a sinner who was lost has been found.

During all His life Jesus was thus patient and merciful to sinners, even to those who were hardened by a long life of sin; He readily suffered the reproach that He was a friend of sinners and publicans.

To the very last moment He showed this same patience and mercy to Judas. Even during the very act of betrayal Jesus spoke kindly to him: "Friend, where to art thou come?" (Matt. 26:50) In one of His parables Jesus symbolized all this love, mercy and patience toward sinners. He calls Himself the Good Shepherd, who has a true heart for His sheep, and who seeks for a sheep that is lost until He finds it. This love and mercy of the Good Shepherd has often been a blessing to you. Perhaps He had to seek you, too, for many years. His mild voice called you when, perhaps, you were mired in sin amidst the thorns and brambles of vice far out in the desert of a godless life. He spoke to you in divers ways through your conscience and through many opportunities which He gave you to recognize the terrible condition of your soul. He did not rest until He had found you; and having found you, He became indeed a good shepherd to you, taking you, the lost sheep, upon His shoulders, and lovingly carrying you back to the true Fold with exceedingly great joy in His Heart. He made it so easy for you by His love, meekness, mercy and patience, that it caused you no humiliation, but rather joy to place your full confidence in Him.

Christian soul, should sin and the pleasures of this world still hold attraction for you, then permit Jesus to find you. Contemplate again the love, patience and mercy of your Saviour and of His most Sacred Heart, and grant Him the joy of carrying you home on His shoulders. Be assured that He is not angry with you. Oh, no; when He arrives at His home, He will call His friends and neighbors, the angels and the saints, the most loving

Mother of God, your patron saint, the faithful souls on earth; and to all these He will say: "Rejoice with Me, because I have found My sheep that was lost" (Luke 15:6). Then you, too, may partake of that heavenly banquet which He has prepared for you in the Blessed Sacrament of the Altar.

DEVOTION FOR COMMUNION

Love for Jesus is enkindled in our hearts by contemplating His life. Call to mind those incidents of the life of Christ which make the greatest appeal to your heart. Before Holy Communion ask yourself these three questions: "Who comes? To whom does He come? Why does He come?"

BEFORE HOLY COMMUNION

Who Comes?

It is Jesus, the Good Shepherd, patient and most merciful toward all His sheep. "I am the good shepherd; and I know Mine, and Mine know Me. As the Father knoweth Me, and I know the Father: and I lay down My life for My sheep" (John 10:14-15). These are the words of Jesus, and with this thought He traversed Palestine for three years to gather together the erring sheep of the house of Israel.

My soul, do you not hear and recognize the voice of the Good Shepherd, who calls and invites you: "Come to Me, all you that labor, and I will refresh you"? (Matt. 11:28)

Faith

O my Jesus, Thou Good Shepherd, who art here present in the Blessed Sacrament that Thou mayest remain the Good Shepherd of Thy flock unto the end of the world, I believe in Thy long-suffering patience and mercy, in Thy unfeigned love for me, Thy lost sheep. Oh, what a pasture Thou hast provided for me! With Thy own precious Flesh and Blood Thou desirest to feed and strengthen my soul, that it may ever remain in Thy grace and never again leave Thee to follow the pleasures of the world. In this sacrament Thou dost open Thy Heart, and from this fountain of life dost grant me all necessary graces. Above all, O Jesus, grant me a living faith in Thy love.

Hope

Because of my faith in Thee, I also place all my trust in Thee, and I give myself to Thee without reserve. Yes, I depend entirely upon Thee and entrust the salvation of my soul to Thee, my watchful Shepherd; for I know: "The Lord is my Shepherd, I shall be wanting in nothing; as long as I belong to His Fold, as long as I hear His voice and answer His call, I shall be secure for time and eternity."

To Whom Does He Come?

He comes to me, the helpless sheep, the foolish creature, who has so often withdrawn from the salutary influence of the Good Shepherd, and who has wandered aimlessly through the desert of life, exposed to the greatest dangers of spiritual starvation. How often has He called me, saying: "Come to My sanctuary, come to Me in the Blessed Sacrament, and strengthen your soul at My Table. You are poor and weak, and exposed to the dangers of sin. Your sins and faults increase in number from day to day and you are entangling yourself more and more in the clinging thorns of tyrannical habits ..." His strong yet tender voice has fascinated my heart. I can no longer withstand the sweet power of His inspirations; I have come, sustained by His grace, to give myself entirely to Him, as He has offered Himself for me.

Humility and Contrition

Who am I, that I should have the inexplicable honor to receive Thee and to have my heart so intimately united with Thine? To think that I, a sinner, a lost sheep of Thy Fold, unworthy to partake of the joys and honor of Thy Banquet, may eat of that Bread of which even the angels are not worthy to eat! Nevertheless, Thou dost invite me to come to Thee, calling me most tenderly. O most merciful Heart of Jesus, accept my sincerest gratitude for this Thy love, and pardon my former ingratitude and coldness. Most sincerely and humbly I again confess my sins to Thee, and I repent of them from the bottom of my heart. I am most sorry, O Lord, that I have hitherto scorned Thy infinite love, and that I offended Thy loving Heart by my past indifference. Heart of Jesus, patient and most merciful, have mercy on me. Amen.

Why Does He Come?
Why did Jesus wait for the sinful woman at the Well of Jacob? Why did He permit Magdalen, the sinner, to anoint His feet? Why? Because He sincerely loves sinners and does not desire that they be punished, but that they be converted; He came to save that which was lost. His Heart is full of the mercy of God. That is the reason He has shown mercy to me and has instituted the sacraments of the Eucharist and Penance; that by these means He might draw me closer to Himself and, as it were, bind me to Himself with golden fetters.

Desire
I take courage, most loving Jesus, to approach Thy holy Table and to receive Holy Communion; not because I am worthy of this grace, but because, in spite of my unworthiness, Thou hast been so good to me. Because I am weak I hasten to Thee, who art all-powerful. Strengthen me, my Good Shepherd! Because I am sinful, I come to Thee, who art most holy; deign to heal the wounds of my soul. Because I am lukewarm and indifferent, I come to Thee, who art the burning furnace of love. Come, oh come my Jesus, and take possession of my heart which desires henceforth to be forever Thine.

AFTER HOLY COMMUNION

Prayer to Jesus, the Good Shepherd
Dearest Shepherd of my soul, Thou didst redeem me at the price of Thy own Flesh and Blood. Thou didst draw me, from my earliest youth, into Thy visible Fold, the holy Catholic Church, through Baptism, and Thou didst nourish and strengthen me with Thy Flesh and Blood. Yes, I was often permitted to rest upon Thy Heart in the greatest intimacy. Oh, how safe do I feel in Thy embrace! Where would it be possible to find a more loving Shepherd than He whom I have now received and of whom I know that He has given His life for me? He it is who endured every trial to draw me nearer to Himself and to protect and cherish me. O Thou Good Shepherd, how happy I am in Thy tender embrace! Only one thing grieves me now, namely, the thought that Thy wishes are not yet fully satisfied. So many

lambs of Thy Fold are still wandering far from Thee, and are enmeshed in the snares of the enemy. Have mercy on them. Remember that Thou didst redeem them by Thy precious Blood. Remember the wearisome journeys of Thy public life, the sermons, parables, exhortations, Thy words of comfort, and lastly Thy bitter Passion and Death. Did Thy ardent zeal deserve no better success? Oh, that all the irreligious, heretics, sinners, lukewarm and fallen-away Catholics would return to Thee! Heart of Jesus, patient and most merciful, have mercy on them; call them back to Thy Fold and touch their hearts with Thy grace … perhaps one more grace will suffice to save their souls.

Most merciful Heart of Jesus, I fear that I, too, forgetting Thy love, may soon fall back again into my former sins, especially into my habitual sin. Do not permit me to seek again the former occasions, but to help me with Thy grace to avoid them. Protect me from Satan, from the seductive world and from myself. Implant into my heart an insatiable desire for greater perfection and love.

Behold, I offer Thee my heart with all its sentiments and impulses, my understanding, my free will, my body and my soul. I consecrate to Thee this First Friday and the entire month. Yes, I wish to consecrate my entire life to Thy service and for Thy greater honor and glory. I offer Thee the hearts of those who are near and dear to me, the hearts of my parents, relatives, benefactors and friends. Do unto them according to Thy great mercy, reward them for all the care, grief and labor of which I was the cause, and grant them the peace of Thy Heart and the joy of a blessed communion with Thee.

Heart of Jesus, have mercy on Thy entire Fold, the holy Catholic Church; grant to Thy representatives on earth the true apostolic zeal which animated Thee, as well as knowledge, wisdom, patience, meekness and humility of heart. Grant to the sheep of Thy Fold a childlike faith, humble obedience and constant loyalty to Thy Church. Lead the erring sheep back to Thy Fold, and through the treasures of Thy grace bring about that soon there may be one Fold and one Shepherd. Amen.

Consecration to the Sacred Heart
O sweetest Heart of Jesus, to Thee the fountain of all blessings, I commit my heart and its tendencies. I commit

myself to Thee without reserve, together with all my sins and faults, especially my love of self, my distrust, my disloyalty, my presumption, my lack of faith and my despair, all my negligence in the fulfillment of the duties of my state of life: that all these may be wiped out by Thy most precious Blood. Henceforth, by Thy grace, I hope to love Thee in thought, word and deed and with all my strength. May I have such faith and hope in Thee that in all my joys and trials I may rely on Thee and be entirely Thine. Grant me the grace to become more and more faithful in Thy service; assist me from day to day, and especially at the hour of my death, to find the safest refuge in Thy most Sacred Heart. Amen.

FIRST FRIDAY IN AUGUST

Heart of Jesus, enriching all who invoke Thee, have mercy on us.

"All the multitude sought to touch Him, for virtue went out from Him, and healed all." (Luke 6:19)

Meditation

My soul, concentrate your attention upon this picture: Jesus, the Son of Man, stands on a small elevation in the plains, and a great multitude of people from all parts of Palestine, in need of consolation and aid of every kind, are crowded around Him. They wish to see this Wonder-worker, to hear this great Teacher, to touch the hem of His garment and be healed by Him. They have a boundless confidence in Him. The words of the Gospel on this point are few but significant: "All the multitude sought to touch Him, for virtue went out from Him, and healed all." Oh, what a triumph for the Heart of Jesus, who pours out impartially the fullness of His power and of heavenly treasures on those who confidently call upon him.

The Heart of Jesus is indeed the treasury which God has opened to mankind. The eternal Father has placed in the Heart of Jesus all His infinite love, power, wisdom and goodness; but He did not seal and barricade it, nor did He place a guard round about it, to prevent our entrance. On the contrary, He desired that as many as possible, yes, all should draw blessings from it. He permitted it to be opened with a lance, and in every Catholic Church in the world He offers its treasures to all who are in need of comfort and salvation. He invites those who are burdened and heavily laden, all who are poor and miserable, to come and receive of the treasures of this Heart.

The afflictions of life are so multi-form: poverty, hunger and thirst, diseases of all kinds, accidents, lightening, hailstorms, earthquakes; and the worries of family life, quarrels, hatred, envy, persecution, the loss of one's good name and reputation, loneliness, afflictions of the heart and adversity - how much misery is called to our minds by the mere mention of some of the evils existing in the world! Christian soul you will find a fitting remedy against these evils in the Sacred Heart of Jesus, because It enriches all who call upon it.

But the greatest and only real evil on earth is sin. The Heart of Jesus contains also the most wonderful balm for this evil. The most beneficial and pleasing strength, but yet the most irresistible, proceeds from the divine Heart and heals all our infirmities.

St. Margaret Mary, who had visions of the very Heart of Jesus, relates: "This divine Heart is an inexhaustible fountain from which issue three constant streams; firstly, the stream of mercy toward all sinners, over whom It pours the spirit of contrition; secondly, the stream of love, which grants to all those in need the necessary aid in their difficulties; thirdly, the stream of love and light for the faithful friends of Jesus, whom He desires to unite with Himself in order to give them His wisdom and His principles. Furthermore, this Heart desires to be a safe refuge and a secure harbor at the hour of death for all those who have honored It during their lives."

No one, therefore, is excluded; and the Sacred Heart requires only one condition, namely, that you call upon It with full confidence. It is understood, of course, that you must be willing to be healed. During His life on earth, Jesus first pardoned the sins of those whom He healed. The greatest of all Physicians always looked upon the root of the ailments, and then in His great mercy He healed them completely.

O my soul, trust confidently in the goodness and mercy of your Savior, and tell Him of your sorrow and your needs, your poverty and tribulations, your lukewarmness and your fear of sacrifices. Seek the presence of the divine Heart as often as you can by meditating earnestly on the treasures of His graces, His gentleness and benevolence, and you will feel the power which flows from this divine Heart.

BEFORE HOLY COMMUNION

Hope

Most gracious Jesus, conscious of my own wretchedness and weakness, I come again to Thee today to receive from Thee what I could not find in the fellowship of my neighbors, namely, a Heart which contains mercy for my weakness and remedies for my ailing soul. O loving Heart of my Savior, Thou art rich to all who invoke Thee. Thou hast words of comfort and strength for those in need, and infinite are the blessings with which Thou dost reward the trust placed in Thee by the sorrowing and sinners. For that reason I feel singularly drawn to Thee, and even now I am filled with the graces which Thy Sacred Heart has poured into my soul. My trust in Thee, O most loving Savior, has grown more fervent because I am permitted not merely to touch the hem of Thy garment, but to receive Thy sacred Person into my heart. Whilst Thou didst sojourn here on earth, all those who came near Thee felt Thy divine power and were healed. In Holy Communion Thou comest in a mysterious and hidden manner, yet with the same Body, now glorified. Not only does a power proceed from Thee into my heart, but Thou Thyself, the Son of God, comest to me with all Thy power, Thy graces and Thy mercy. Thou comest with Thy Body and Thy Soul, Thy Humanity and Divinity. I have boundless hope in Thee, because I am convinced that I shall receive from Thee whatever is good for my soul.

Sacred Heart of Jesus, I trust in Thee. (Indulgence: 300 days. Plenary once a month.)

Faith

O Jesus, Thou didst always demand, from those whom Thou didst wish to heal, faith in Thy almighty power and love; and after they had been freed from their ailments Thou didst dismiss them with the words: "Go in peace, they faith hath made thee whole." Behold I, too, firmly believe in Thy omnipotence and love, through which Thou art present in the Blessed Sacrament of the Altar. I, too, believe that Thou, to whom all power was given in heaven and on earth, hast granted the power to Thy Apostles and to all their successors, the bishops and priests of Thy Church, to change bread into Thy sacred Body and wine into Thy precious Blood. I believe that Thou wilt come to me today with Thy Body and Soul, Thy Humanity and Divinity, to be my Food: thus to heal my infirmities and my weakness, and to hear and answer my prayers. Heart of Jesus, strengthen my faith!

Offering

Divine Savior, Thine eyes penetrate the innermost recesses of my soul. Thou perceivest more clearly than I myself my many needs, the weight of my sins and my lack of merits. Thou knowest the frailty of my nature. Behold, I offer Thee all that I am and possess. I beg Thee to take charge of me; cleanse, heal, comfort, strengthen and purify me in the furnace of Thy loving Heart; enkindle in me a love like Thine, so that henceforth I may always please Thee and be entirely Thine.

I offer Thee this Holy Communion in atonement for the sins of my past life and as a reparation for the ingratitude of mankind. I offer it to Thee for myself and my relatives, for my friends and benefactors, and for all those who seek Thy aid in their trials and temptations. I offer it to Thee for those who have not yet learned of Thy power and love and therefore do not call upon Thee. May this Holy Communion help to increase Thy honor and the knowledge of Thy love.

"May the Sacred Heart of Jesus be loved everywhere." (Indulgence: 300 days each time.)

Desire

Most loving Jesus, whose joy it is to be among the children of men, to aid them in their weakness and to heal their ailments, my heart yearns for Thee, my soul desires to receive Thee. Come, oh, come to me. I invite Thee with the sincere intention of giving Thee as much joy as I possibly can. Thou art infinitely rich in heavenly treasures and graces, and canst easily supply what is lacking in my heart. Come, O divine Physician, and heal my ailing soul. Come, Thou rich Guest, and aid me in my poverty and want. It is true, O Lord, that I am not worthy to receive Thee into my soul, but say only the word, and my soul shall be healed! Amen.

Thanksgiving After Holy Communion

O my Jesus, permit me to greet Thee in this, the most blessed embrace of my life. Thee, who dost now refresh me with Thy presence! In silent adoration I desire to enjoy Thy substantial presence in my soul, in union with Thy most ardent, tender and blessed love. O Lord, my God, and my Savior! O God of love, Thou art truly within my heart. Jesus in me, and I in Him. Jesus the expectation of the prophets, the bliss of all the angels, O Jesus, my Jesus! Grant that I may adore Thee, love Thee and praise Thee with all my heart and soul. Oh, that all my thoughts and desires, yes, all my strivings, were centered in Thee alone; would that my heart were forever one with Thine, so that it would henceforth see, desire, think and love nothing but Thee. Thou has given Thyself entirely to me and art now substantially present in my soul, and I am impelled to say with the spouse in the Canticle of Canticles: "I found him whom my soul loveth; I hold him: and I will not let him go" 3:4). No, nothing shall separate me from Thee again, my Jesus; not my formed unfaithfulness and sins, not my former coldness and lack of decision, not my formed indifference; nothing in the world, no temptations, no trial nor misery, no labor nor persecution, nothing in the world shall separate me from Thee, with Whom I am now united in such an inexpressibly blessed, sweet and intimate manner.

O Jesus, hear my fervent prayer; direct Thine eyes upon me, enrich me with Thy grace, and in this Holy Communion unite me inseparable with Thy loving Heart. Grant that henceforth I may remain true to Thee forever. Even as a starving beggar pleads for crumbs of bread, so I, at this moment, long for the graces that flow from Thy love. With burning desire I call to Thee: "With my whole heart have I sought after Thee: let me not stray from They Commandments" (Ps. 188:10). I shall not hinder the effects of Thy grace, O Lord. No, with all my heart I desire Thee.

With St. Ignatius I call upon Thee to take from me my freedom, my understanding, my free will and everything that I possess; only grant me Thy love, and I shall be rich beyond comparison. Now that I possess Thee, O Jesus, all my desires are fulfilled. Would that I had the fervor of the seraphim to thank Thee for this immeasurable grace! Oh, could I but express my love and gratitude toward Thee in the words spoken by Thy great saints whenever they had the joy of receiving Thee! I thank Thee with the gratitude of all the angels and saints, because Thou didst humiliate Thyself in coming to me, the most unworthy of all Thy creatures, to favor me with the presence of Thy Divinity and Humanity. I thank Thee, my dearest Jesus, for this wondrous grace. I thank Thee for all the Holy Communions which have been received throughout the world for Thy honor and glory. I hope that Thy grace will bear fruit a hundredfold in my soul, and that I may never fail to prove, by faithfulness to Thee, my desire to be forever Thine. (Renew your good resolutions, especially to keep this day holy by greater devotion, recollection and good works.)

Oh, what a powerful remedy is Holy Communion! To understand this more fully I need but to remember that one Holy Communion, received with the proper disposition, can make me a saint. O my sweetest Jesus, grant that I may be wholly united with Thee by this Holy Communion so that I may at last begin to live only with Thee and for Thee. I desire henceforth to think with Thy mind, so see with Thy eyes, to hear with Thy ears, to speak with Thy tongue, to labor with Thy hands, and to love God and my neighbor according to Thy Heart. In this Holy Communion Thou didst give me Thy Body and Soul, Thy Divinity and Humanity; live, then, entirely in me, O Jesus, so that I may truly say with the Apostle: "I live now not I, but Christ liveth in me."

May this and every Holy Communion of my life be to me a pledge of eternal salvation; and at the hour of death, may Thy most Sacred Heart through this mysterious union be united to mine until my soul leaves my body and I am called to the eternal feast of the Lamb.

O Jesus, hear and strengthen me, sanctify, protect and save me. Bless all the faculties of my soul, so that I may always, in every thought, word and deed, give glory and honor to Thee. With this intention and with a living faith, a firm hope and a most sincere love, I now pronounce Thy sweet and holy Name: Jesus. Amen.

Act of Homage to the Eucharistic Heart of Jesus
Eucharistic Heart of my God, living and beating under the veil of the Sacred Species, I adore Thee.

Moved afresh with love for the immense benefit of the divine Eucharist, penetrated with sorrow for my ingratitude, I humble and annihilate myself in the still greater abyss of Thy mercies.

Thou didst choose me from childhood; Thou didst not despise my infirmity; Thou didst descend into my poor heart, and, giving it happiness and peace, didst invite it to mutual love. But I have lost all by being unfaithful to Thee, O Jesus, My Lord. I have allowed my spirit to become dissipated and my heart to become cold; I have listened to my own voice and have forgotten Thee.

Thou wouldst have been my guide, my counselor, the protector of my life; and I, allowing my passions to destroy the sweet attraction of Thy presence, have lost sight of Thee and forgotten Thee.

In the salutary trials of my probation, in times of joy and consolation, in my difficulties and necessities, instead of having recourse to Thee, I have gone after creatures, and have forgotten Thee.

I have forgotten Thee in deserted tabernacles, where Thy love languishes; in the churches of towns, where Thou art outraged; in the hearts of the indifferent and sacrilegious, and also in my own heart, O Jesus.

Eucharistic Heart of my Savior, the delight of my first Communion and the days of my fidelity, I surrender to Thee. Return, oh, return to me; draw me to Thyself anew. Pardon me again but this one time, and I shall hope for everything from the strength of Thy love.

Glorious Archangel St. Michael, and thou, O beloved disciple St. John, offer to Jesus this my act of reparation, and be merciful to me. Amen. (Indulgence: 500 days each time.)

Prayer to St. Margaret Mary

Thrice-blessed virgin, who wast especially chose by Jesus to proclaim the infinite love of His most Sacred Heart for men, and thus to awaken among the faithful a great devotion to It, help me to honor this most Sacred Heart with sincere love, and to take refuge in It in all temptations, trials and necessities; so that thus I may partake of Its manifold blessings. Amen.

FIRST FRIDAY IN SEPTEMBER

Heart of Jesus, our peace and reconciliation, have mercy on us.

"I will not condemn thee. Go, and sin no more." (John 8:11)

Meditation

The prophet Isaias called the promised Messiah the Prince of Peace. Indeed, humility and meekness, kindness and mercy, are His scepter and His crown. His nobility and majesty weigh only upon the proud, the Pharisee and the hypocrite; the poor and the sinner find the source of their faith and trust in Him. He is a ruler of hearts. He requires neither pomp nor the show of power like kings of this earth; He needs but to open His Heart, and the powers of darkness flee in confusion while, drawn to Him by the beauty of His Heart, the humble and the weak, as also the contrite sinner, hasten to Him, seeking and finding peace and salvation.

During Christ's public life an adulteress was taken in sin. According to the Mosaic law, though not according to the law of Romans, she was guilty of death. Jesus, the King of the World, was to pass judgment upon her. Those who accused her, knowing the law, proudly brought her to Jesus to tempt Him. Sneeringly they asked: "But what sayest Thou?" How artfully they put their question. If Jesus confirmed their judgment and agreed to have her stoned, He decided against the Roman law and would be an enemy of Caesar; if He ruled that she should be set free, His decision would be contrary to the Mosaic law and He would be an enemy of the people. They did not know of the new law, the law of the merciful Heart of Jesus, which condemns only the obstinate sinner, while the penitent sinner receives pardon. Jesus judged according to this law. He stooped to the ground, and with His finger wrote in the sand. What did He write? The Pharisees watched Him, not knowing that He was writing their own sins. Jesus therefore said to them: "He that is without sin among you, let him first cast a stone at her" (John 8:7). They understood then the meaning of His writing. And as Jesus again began to write, "they went out one by one, beginning at the eldest."

Jesus, lifting up Himself, was alone with the sinful woman.

Their eyes met. What a meeting this was! The Most Holy One and the sinner; God and His ungrateful creature. Without witnesses … alone. It was one of those sacred moments in which the Heart of Jesus beats in mercy for the sinner, and the Saviour offers him the hand of peace speaking the pardoning words: "Neither will I condemn thee. Go, and sin no more."

Dear Christian, reflect for a moment on your own life, and recall the errors of the past. You will find many moments when you were alone with your Saviour; you, with sin in your heart, and He, full of love and mercy; you, restless, fearful and distracted in the knowledge of your sinfulness, and He, looking upon you with eyes radiant with peace and mercy. A burden was lifted from your heart; in confession, and especially in Holy Communion, you found the plentitude of peace and reconciliation. Therefore, in times of temptations, spiritual unrest and anxiety, take refuge in the Sacred Heart of Jesus, and say with confidence: "Heart of Jesus, our peace and reconciliation, have mercy on us."

The Heart of Jesus obtains for us not only peace within our souls, but peace with the world as well. His favorite greeting to the Apostles was: "Peace be with you"; and on the evening before He died and said to them: "Peace I leave with you, My peace I give unto you" (John 14:27). During His sermon on the Mount He proclaimed the peacemakers blessed, because they would be called children of God. This same holy peace of God, peace in families, congregations and nations, Jesus has promised anew, through St. Margaret Mary, to all who venerate His most Sacred Heart.

Let us, then, be true adorers of the Sacred Heart, by imitating His love for peace and often praying for the gift of peace.

"Heart of Jesus, our peace and reconciliation, have mercy on us."

DEVOTION FOR COMMUNION

Holy Communion makes us one with Jesus, the living, consoling, loving, forgiving, assisting and healing Jesus. Be assured that He can and will help you, too.

BEFORE HOLY COMMUNION

Adoration

Jesus, my Saviour, I adore Thee in the Blessed Sacrament as the God of peace and the loving Ruler of hearts. With deepest reverence I believe that Thou art the omniscient Judge, who knows every secret of my heart, and to whom not one of my thoughts nor desires, nor any of my words, deeds and intentions is unknown. I adore Thee with all my love and confidence, and firmly believe that Thou dost not desire the death of the sinner, but that he be converted and live.

Thou knowest the needs of my soul. Thou seest the temptations which trouble my heart and the passions which threaten to rob it of Thy peace. Thou knowest, too, the many dangers which surround me, how the powers of darkness attack me in order to separate me from Thee. The spirit of selfishness, pride, envy and discord is rampant in the world and endeavors to suppress the voice of the Prince of Peace: "Peace be with you."

Humility and Contrition

O Jesus, the number of my transgressions and sins is exceedingly great, but the number of my merits and good works is small indeed. If Thou hadst not invited sinners to come to Thee, I would never dare to approach Thy holy Table. Now that I have come, O Jesus, speak the words of Thy almighty power, which will wipe out my sins; speak the word of love, which remits the punishment due to my sins. Oh, speak the words of peace: "Thy sins are forgiven thee; go, and sin no more."

I am willing to suffer anything rather than commit sin again. Dearest Saviour, I regret and lament my sins from the bottom of my heart, because by them I have grieved and offended Thy loving Heart; because by them I have rebelled against Thy heavenly Father, my Lord and my Creator, and have deserved temporal and eternal punishment. I am sorry for having committed sin, because by it I have destroyed the grace of the Holy Ghost in my soul and lost the peace of the children of God. May I henceforth hate, detest and avoid sin and seek only Thy peace.

"My Jesus, mercy." (Indulgence: 300 days. Plenary once a month.)

"Sweetest Jesus, be to me not a judge but a Saviour."
(Indulgence: 300 days. Plenary once a month.)

Desire

Almighty God, is it possible that Thou, whom I adore in this humble species of bread, hast hidden Thyself in this form to come to me and unite Thyself with me? Can it be true that Thou, whom the heavens cannot contain, livest under the species of bread because Thou desirest to be with me always? O incomprehensible Goodness! How could I ever believe in such a miracle of love if Thou didst not convince me by Thy own words? That Thou should so humble Thyself as to come into my mouth, to lie on my tongue, and to enter into my body, seems still more incredible. And yet Thou desirest to do this; in order to induce me to receive Thee, Thou dost promise me many wonderful blessings. Why, O God of Love, do I lack understanding to know Thy mercy; why is my heart so cold that I do not feel this mercy; why does my tongue not praise Thy goodness? Thou art my God, who hast created me and made me the object of Thy love. The angels never grow weary of beholding Thee; should not I, then, long to possess Thee? Therefore, I open my heart to receive Thee, O most amiable Saviour, because Thy goodness permits it and my many needs impel me to unite myself with Thee.

Come, O my divine Sun, come to me, who am lost in the utter darkness of ignorance and sin; come to dispel this darkness, and grant that the light of Thy knowledge may again enlighten my understanding. Come, O most amiable Saviour. Thou didst abandon Thyself to strange hands, in order to save me from eternal punishment; come Thou, O Jesus, release me from the fetters of my sins and grant me the freedom of Thy loyal children. O Thou most tender, meek and faithful Friend, come to my aid. My soul, which Thou lovest so much, lies prostrate before Thee. O my Saviour, who knowest all things, Thou knowest also my helplessness. Through Thy incomparable love, and by Thy teachings, I pray Thee, come to my assistance. Come to me, and never permit me to be separated from Thee again. Come Thou life of my soul, Thou, my only support. Come, Thou Bread of the angels, and be my Food.

Come, then, my God and my All, and grant new life to my

languishing soul; for my soul longs for Thee who art the motive of its love and the fountain of its life. Jesus, my Love, I conjure Thee to take possession of all my thoughts, and by the power of Thy love to release my heart from all worldly desires. O Lord, wound my heart so deeply that it will desire nothing worldly nor human, but will be filled with love for Thee alone. Yes, do Thou reign in my heart forever. Amen.

AFTER HOLY COMMUNION

Thanksgiving
"My soul doth magnify the Lord, and my spirit hath rejoiced in God my Saviour" (Luke 1:46-47), because He has regarded the humility of my soul, and has had mercy on me. After pardoning my sins in the sacrament of Penance, He now gives the clearest proof of His love by coming to me in Holy Communion and uniting Himself most intimately with me. A thousand thanks for this unmerited grace.

Oh, could I but express my deep gratitude in words more fitting! I desire to greet Thee with the same reverence and love with which Thy holy Mother received Thee from the Holy Ghost on the day of the Annunciation; with a heart as pure and immaculate as Thine own, and by a life of such virtue as would make me like unto Thee. This would indeed be the highest gratitude. But, alas, how far removed from perfection is my gratitude for Thy gifts! How weak am I in the virtue of self-denial, in overcoming my pride, self-love, weakness and impatience. On the other hand, it is so difficult for me to imitate Thy holy zeal, love of neighbor, patience, meekness, humility and mortification. O most sacred Body of my Lord, be Thou the food and strength of my soul, that I may conquer triumphantly the inordinate passions of my human nature; and Thou, O most precious Blood of the immaculate Lamb, purify me from all stains of sin; inflame my heart with the fire of Thy love, so that henceforth it may love only Thee.

I pray also, as Thou desirest me to do, for those who are near and dear to me; for my parents, superiors, brothers and sisters, relatives, friends and benefactors, for the living and the dead. Bestow upon them the peace of Thy Heart. Grant to the living a holy desire for the peace of a good conscience, and give to the departed the peace of heaven.

Heart of Jesus, our peace and reconciliation, have mercy especially on sinners, infidels and heretics, and give them the peace which the world cannot give. Furthermore, I beg of Thee to grant peace and concord to Thy holy Church and to all Christian princes and rulers. Imbue them with the spirit of peace and conciliation, that Thy Kingdom may expand, and that soon all nations of the earth may be united under Thy benign scepter.

"Divine Heart of Jesus, convert sinners, save the dying, set free the holy souls in purgatory." (Indulgence: 300 days.)

"Sacred Heart of Jesus, Thy Kingdom come." (Indulgence: 300 days.)

Prayer in Honor of St. Mary Magdalen

O most gracious Jesus, Thou didst not repulse the sinner Magdalen, when she approached Thee to kiss Thy feet, to wash them with her tears, and to anoint them. Behold, in heartfelt sorrow I cast myself at Thy feet and beg of Thee to pardon all my transgressions as Thou didst forgive Mary Magdalen. I would gladly anoint Thy sacred feet, seeking only to honor Thee and to offer all my honor as a sacrifice to Thee. O St. Magdalen, pray for me, that I may not cease to deplore my sins as long as I live, and that I may never neglect to honor my divine Saviour; so that I, even as thou, may enjoy heavenly glory. Amen.

Offering

Divine Heart of Jesus, inexhaustible fountain of love and mercy, Thou hast given proof of Thy infinite love for man in an ineffable manner through Thy cruel Passion and Death and by the institution of the Blessed Sacrament of the Altar. Therefore it is meet and just that all men should love and adore Thee above all things. Hence it is sad, indeed, to see that from many, and even from me, Thou receivest only indifference and ingratitude. This must fill Thy Heart, O sweetest Jesus, with deep sorrow, but mine with shame and remorse. I assure Thee, my Jesus, that I am most heartily sorry for my ingratitude, coldness and indifference. O most gracious Heart, O Heart of my God, who alone hast power to pardon sinners, forgive me all my sins; enlightened and strengthened by Thy grace, I declare myself willing and prepared to restore Thy honor and to amend my life.

If I have hitherto refused to love Thee as I ought, I now declare myself entirely and forever Thine. Oh, how I welcome this blessed moment, which Thou, most loving Heart of Jesus, hast granted to me, this moment, in which I am permitted to dedicate my love and my whole heart to Thee alone. Take them for time and eternity. And as Thou hast now granted me the grace to make this offering, I beg of Thee that, whenever it may please Thee, Thou mayest bestow upon me the crown of eternal life. Amen.

FIRST FRIDAY IN OCTOBER

Heart of Jesus, salvation of those who trust in Thee, have mercy on us.

"Why are you fearful, O ye of little faith?" (Matt. 8:26)

Meditation

Who does not know the story of the ship which was tossed about in a terrible storm, a toy of the raging elements, which threatened to sink it any moment? It was not by chance that this storm arose. The extraordinary Man who was sleeping in the boat had foreseen the tempest. In spite of this, perhaps because of it, He had boarded the fragile bark. But the poor disciples! Free from all misgivings, they had gone out into the very danger of death; and now they battled for their lives. But Jesus slept.

What a contrast between the stormy sea, the howling wind, the frightened Apostles and the calm countenance of the sleeping Saviour! In this you will discern an important lesson of the Heart of Jesus. The apparent indifference of Jesus teaches you how trivial are the dangers and trials of this world in comparison with those which threaten the salvation of souls; because where a soul is to be saved Jesus does not sleep, but seeks after the lost sheep until He has found it and freed it from the snares of Satan.

But Jesus slept. Does He not know the distress of His Apostles? He does know it, and His Heart is awake and is only waiting to hear their call for aid. When finally the danger of death became imminent, they did what they should have done in the very beginning of the storm; they called upon Jesus, who alone could help them. And behold, immediately the divine power of the Heart of Jesus becomes manifest: "Then rising up, He commanded the wind, and the sea, and there came a great calm" (Matt. 8:26). The Heart of Jesus had saved them. It need not surprise you, then, that the Apostles, after receiving their mission to teach all nations, were unafraid of the dangers of life and of the persecutions to which their enemies subjected them. This miracle which they had witnessed gave them forever an unlimited trust in the Heart of Jesus.

Dear Christian, in times of need and distress you, too, must place your trust in the Heart of the Saviour. You will not be spared the storms from within, arising from the depths of your passionate heart. How often do arrogance, pride and obstinacy disturb the quiet of your heart! How enticingly does the lust of the flesh sometimes assault you, so that you almost lose your spiritual balance! And what tyrannical despots are such passions as gluttony, avarice, ambition and inordinate love of honor and admiration! Lastly, what storms are raging in your heart when anger and impatience strive for mastery over you!

O poor, weak human heart, do not lose courage during such tempests in your soul; remember the storm on Lake Genesareth, and feel assured that your Saviour is near you; He is only asleep, and desires you to call Him with childlike trust in His goodness. His rich and powerful Heart can and desires to save you. Call upon Him: Lord, save me, I perish! Heart of Jesus, salvation of those who trust in Thee, have mercy on me.

The small ship of the Apostles on Lake Genesareth reminds us also of the ship of Peter, our holy Catholic Church, which has always been exposed to the powers of darkness, and even in our day has to fight the severest storms. How many there are who lose faith in her power of resistance because they do not know the omnipotence of the Sacred Heart of Jesus. Why did Jesus wait until our times to reveal His Heart, if not in order to give strength to the weak, to save those of little faith? How foolish it would be to lose courage just at this time when Jesus is roused, as it were, and rises up to save His Church. Persevere in your trust in the Sacred Heart of Jesus, which will never be separated from the Church. Did He not say: "Behold I am with you all days, even to the consummation of the world" (Matt. 28:20)? "Have confidence, I have conquered the world" (John 16:33), and indeed, the Heart of Jesus has consummated a perfect union between Itself and the Church; and therefore the gates of hell shall never prevail against the Church, and all its members who trust in the Sacred Heart of Jesus shall be saved.

DEVOTION FOR COMMUNION

It is not a law of man, but of God, that every Catholic has an inalienable right to receive Holy Communion and may approach the Table of the Lord daily if he desires to do so. Be thankful for this right, and make use of it as often as possible.

Prayer to the Sacred Heart of Jesus
Most gracious and powerful Jesus, salvation of all who trust in Thee, behold, I come to Thee to confess my needs and the anxiety of my soul. O Lord, help me, I perish! The dangers which threaten my soul are so many and so terrifying that I feel too weak to persevere in the constant battle. Yes, if Thou doest no come to my aid, I shall certainly perish. Through the grace of the holy sacrament of Penance Thou didst enter the ship of my soul spiritually. Oh, come to me now with Thy Body and Thy Soul, and bring with Thee Thy living Heart, Thy powerful and gracious Heart, so that joy, peace, contentment and bliss may take possession of it. Awake, O Jesus, and come to my aid; grant me strength and courage; calm the waves of passion and desires which trouble me; command the storms which assail my soul from without; keep far from me the temptations of the world, and grant me that wonderful peace of Thy Heart.

Faith
Divine Saviour, I firmly believe in Thy real presence in the most holy Sacrament of the Altar. I believe that Thou art here present in a living manner. Although Thou givest no outward manifestation of Thy living presence, although Thou art here apparently dead, nevertheless my faith tells me that here Thy Heart beats with burning love for me, that Thy eyes see me and Thy ears hear the voice of my distressed heart. I believe that Thou livest here solely for me and for all those who need Thy assistance, because it is only for this reason that Thou desirest to remain among us. Strengthen my faith in Thy real presence. Never permit me to doubt this truth, least of all when my soul is weakened from the constant battle with the evil spirit, and especially when it must pass through its last and most serious test. Then may my faith in Thy loving presence enable me to find the way to the secure refuge of Thy Sacred Heart. Most Sacred Heart of Jesus, I believe in Thy love for me.

Hope
How could I possibly be faint-hearted or lose courage, when Thou, my beloved Jesus, art so near, and when I am about to be

perfectly united with Thee? Through Thee I can do all things; because Thou art my strength, my comfort, my light and my refuge in the dangers of this life. I trust entirely in Thee, for Thou hast encouraged me by Thy words: "Have confidence, I have conquered the world" (John 16:33). By the power of Thy word Thou hast commanded the storm and the sea, and there came a great calm. Manifest the fullness of Thy divine power in my also by commanding the enemies of my salvation. Speak but the word, and all those who wish me evil and strive to injure my soul will be confounded.

"Sacred Heart of Jesus, I trust in Thee." (Indulgence: 300 days. Plenary once a month.)

Love

O Jesus, most worthy of all love, whom even the angels and saints in heaven cannot love as much as Thou deservest, hearken to the voice of Thy most wretched creature, who desires to tell Thee of his great love for Thee. I love Thee as my most generous Father, who gave me the life of grace through excruciating pains on the cross; I love Thee as my Brother, who out of love for me became man in order to be able to labor, suffer and die for me; I love Thee as my Friend, who knows all the needs of my heart and has compassion for me, who shares with me the trials and joys of life, and who is my Protector in times of danger and my Saviour when I have sinned. Oh, I love Thee as the Spouse of my soul, whose Heart is inflamed with love for me, and who makes every sacrifice to manifest that love. I love Thee as my intimate Companion, who lives in the tabernacle day and night, so that I may call upon Him at any time and trustingly confide my sorrows to Him.

O incomprehensible love of the Heart of Jesus, I adore Thee, I praise and glorify Thee, and I marvel at Thy goodness. I long for Thee, and I consecrate myself to Thee. O heavenly Love, I love Thee above all things, because Thou art infinitely perfect, sublime, and inexpressibly beautiful. I will forget myself that I may love only Thee. O Love, I am Thine, and Thine I wish to be forever and ever. Amen.

"Sweet Heart of Jesus, be my love." (Indulgence: 300 days.)

Prayer to Mary

Mary, thou powerful and gracious Queen of Heaven, at this moment, when I am about to receive thy divine Son into my heart, I recommend myself to the care of thy motherly love and solicitude. Assist me to receive worthily this Holy Communion. Thou purest Queen of Virgins, thou Immaculate Spouse of God, help me to make another act of perfect contrition, so that my heart and soul may be truly freed from every stain of sin. Then I shall be prepared to receive thy beloved Son from thy motherly hands, take Him lovingly into my heart, and remember thee gratefully. O Mary, Mother of the Redeemer, our Mediatrix, obtain for me the grace to unite myself inseparably with thy Jesus, to become more and more like unto Him, to love Him forevermore and to live and die in His love.

Contrition and Humility

Most amiable Jesus, with my whole heart I again beg of Thee to pardon all my sins; wash them away with Thy precious Blood, and fill my heart with true contrition and a burning love. Would that I had never grieved Thy Sacred Heart. Would that I had always lived according to Thy holy will. Heart, then, at least now, O beloved Jesus, the humble pleading of Thy sinful creature: "O Lord, I am not worthy that Thou shouldst enter into my heart, but say only the word, and my soul shall be healed."

AFTER HOLY COMMUNION

Thanksgiving and Oblation

I welcome Thee into my heart, most amiable Jesus, my life, my refuge and my salvation. I welcome Thee in the name of the Father, who has given Thee to me; in the name of the Holy Spirit, who, in union with Thee, desires to sanctify me. I welcome Thee in the name of Thy holy Mother, in the name of the angels and saints, as well as in the name of those poor souls in purgatory who hope for salvation through this Holy Communion. I welcome Thee in the name of Thy holy Church and of all the faithful in the world. I welcome Thee for all those who do not receive Thee because they know not the sweetness of Thy love.

May through this Holy Communion a ray of Thy grace enter the hearts of sinners! O Thou almighty God, Thou Prince of

Peace, Thou Saviour and Redeemer of all the faithful, be eternally welcome within my heart. Would that I were possessed of all the flames of love which have ever been enkindled by Thy Heart, so that I might pay Thee homage and render Thee thanksgiving for this incomprehensible grace and blessing of Thy visit to me.

I wish to thank Thee, O Jesus, not only in words, but also in deed, by consecrating myself entirely to Thee:

"Take, O Lord, all my liberty. Receive my memory, understanding and entire will. Thou hast bestowed on me whatever I have or possess; I return it all to Thee, and leave it entirely to the guidance of Thy holy will. Only grant me Thy love and Thy grace, and I shall be rich enough and shall ask for nothing more." (Indulgence: 3 years each time. Plenary once a month.)

Petition

My Lord and my God, effect in me by Thy grace what Thou didst intend to accomplish in coming to me. Thou didst come to unite Thyself intimately with me, to make me share in all the merits which Thou hast gained by Thy life and death, to enrich me with all the treasures of grace through Thy Sacred Heart, to sanctify my body and my soul, and finally, to teach me the way of a saintly life. Thou didst come to me to reveal to angels and men and to all creatures how amiable and munificent Thou art, and how earnestly desirous to grant me Thy most precious blessings. Thou didst come in order to glorify Thy name and to have the joy of beholding Thy Blood and Thy sufferings bearing abundant fruit in my soul. Can it be possible, then, that Thou, who never dost anything in vain, shouldst come from heaven to this earth, shouldst work so many miracles and make such great preparations without effect? Therefore I beg of Thee, my God, Thou greatest good, wisdom and power, do not fail to accomplish the purpose of Thy visit. Unite the height of Thy perfection with the abyss of my misery, the infinite depths of Thy mercy with the abyss of my necessities, Thy awe-inspiring omnipotence with the abyss of my weakness, Thy infinite wealth with my abject poverty. Shower the merits of Thy life and death upon me so that my body and soul and all my thoughts, words and deeds may be sanctified.

My dearest Jesus, present in my heart, Thou knowest all my needs. Thou knowest that without Thee I can do nothing, but united with Thee I can do all things. Thou knowest that I am not humble, kind nor patient; that I am too weak to resist any temptation without being able to rise again without Thy assistance. O Thou, my love, have compassion on my wretchedness. Because of Thy visit in my soul, grant me the virtue of humility and a thorough understanding of my nothingness, a delicate purity of heart and mind, as well as the gift of Thy love in the highest degree, so that I may love Thee, with all my heart. Enrich me with the grace of perfect harmony with Thy holy will and also with the strength and perseverance which are so necessary to assist me in overcoming my evil inclinations. Above all, O God, pardon my past offenses against Thee and grant me the grace never to commit them again. Teach me to do all things with a pure intention and to place small value on creatures, so that henceforth I may love nothing but Thee. Bestow upon me the necessary wisdom and prudence for the proper fulfillment of the duties of my state in life, especially patience in bearing whatever may be bitter and disagreeable to me.

Most holy Virgin, my amiable Mother, I beg of thee to give thanks to the adorable holy Trinity for the great honor which was bestowed upon me today by the coming of Jesus into my heart. O Mary, thank thy divine Son for me and beg of Him that He may hear and answer all my petitions because of the love I have for thee.

"O Jesus, who dost live in Mary, come and live in Thy servants in the spirit of Thine own holiness, in the fullness of Thy power, in the reality of Thy virtues, in the perfection of Thy ways, in the communion of Thy mysteries; have Thou dominion over every adverse power, in Thine own spirit, to the glory of the Father. Amen."

Consecration to the Sacred Heart
O most adorable and sweet Heart of my Jesus, constantly inflamed with love for mankind, ever open to shower Thy treasures upon us; O Heart, always filled with compassion for us in our trials, always desirous to bestow Thy graces and blessings upon us and to come to us in Holy Communion; O Heart, ever

ready to be our refuge, our dwelling-place and our paradise on earth, is it possible that in return for all this kindness Thou dost receive from the hearts of men only thoughtlessness, disrespect and hardness of heart? Thou lovest truly, but Thou dost not receive love in return. Many do not even know Thy love; others reject it or turn a deaf ear when Thou speakest to their hearts.

In order to repair this ignominy and ingratitude, and also to preserve myself as far as I am able from the danger of falling into the same misfortune, I offer Thee, O Jesus, my heart and all its emotions. Henceforth I desire to forget myself and all my own interests, and thus to remove all obstacles that may render my approach to Thy Heart more difficult. Thou has deigned to open Thy Heart to me, and I have a great desire to enter It, so that I may live and die inflamed with Thy love. Amen.

FIRST FRIDAY IN NOVEMBER

Heart of Jesus, fountain of life and holiness, have mercy on us.

"I am the vine; you are the branches: he that abideth in Me, and I in him, the same beareth much fruit." (John 15:5)

Meditation

It was after the Last Supper. The Apostles had received their first Holy Communion. Judas had just left to carry out his satanic plan. As if the departure of the traitor had brought comfort to the Heart of Jesus, He at once began to speak to the Apostles with the greatest intimacy. He knew that He was among His own. By means of their first Holy Communion He had united Himself with them and they with Him in a most intimate love. It was as if the greatest desire that He had cherished from all eternity in the bosom of His Father had been satisfied at last. "Now is the Son of Man glorified," He said, "and God is glorified in Him . . . Little children, yet a little while I am with you . . . A new commandment I give unto you: that you love one another, as I have loved you" (John 13:31-34).

Jesus then continued, as we read in the Gospel according to St. John, to pour out His Heart to His Apostles. He recounted again all the blessings that He was about to leave to them as a precious legacy. He spoke of the Home of His Father, where He was to build mansions for them, of the benevolence of the Father and of the Holy Ghost, the Comforter. He consoled them by promising them His peace, that peace of heart which the world cannot give.

He then illustrated by the parable of the vine how He would give to His Apostles and to all who believe in Him His own divine life, the wealth of His grace and true sanctity through a spiritual and corporal union with them. This twofold union between Him and the Apostles had already become a fact. He was in them and they in Him through sanctifying grace and through the real presence of His Flesh and Blood. Therefore He continued: "Abide in Me and I in you . . . I am the vine; you the branches . . . as the branch cannot bear fruit of itself, unless it abide in the vine, so neither can you, unless you abide in Me" (John 15:4,5).

What a profound parable! It teaches us that we can receive and preserve the supernatural life of grace only if we are and remain united with Christ in faith and love. Separated from Him by sin, we cannot share in the rejuvenating strength of life which flows from His Heart, and therefore cannot bear fruits of sanctity. His Heart is indeed the source of life and holiness.

"I am the vine, you the branches." Thoughts not understood by the world. But what can the world understand about God? Jesus explicitly excluded the world from the priestly prayer which He recited at the close of His discourse after the Last Supper, when He said: "I pray not for the world" (John 17:9). He prayed only for His Apostles and for all His future followers: "Holy Father, keep them in Thy name whom Thou hast given Me; that they may be one, as We also are . . . They are not of the world as I also am not of the world. Sanctify them in truth . . . and for them do I sanctify Myself, that they also may be sanctified in truth" (John 17).

It is the Heart's desire of Jesus, not that His disciples find pleasure in the world, nor that the world love them, but that in spite of the world they may become holy. In order that they may fully understand Him and know whom they should choose as their ideal, He said: "For them do I sanctify Myself" (John 17:19). By His own most holy life Jesus laid the foundation of holiness for all His followers. He is the fountain of all holiness and the ideal for those who strive after it. He is the model and the first-born of all the saints. He is the vine, they are the branches; they live in Him, and from His Heart they draw all graces and virtues; from Him they learn humility, meekness, patience, friendliness, obedience, self-denial, mortification, love of the cross, and true love of God and their neighbor; and because all virtues become active in the soul through the Sacred Heart of Jesus, we may truly say that this Heart remains for all times the fountain of holiness.

The saints knew this well; for this reason they fostered the most intimate union with the Heart of Jesus through their perfect love of Him, and tried, by constant meditations on His life, to learn more and more about their Ideal and to follow in His footsteps. Now they enjoy the reward of their efforts. And what a great reward! After the Last Supper Jesus had prayed for all of them: "Father, I will that where I am, they also whom Thou hast given Me may be with Me; that they may see My glory" (John 17:24). This prayer was heard. Indeed, no eye has seen, nor ear heard, neither has it entered into the heart of man, what God has prepared for those who have honored and loved the most Sacred Heart of Jesus. Now they behold this Heart, the most sublime masterpiece of the Creator, the Heart of the Lamb which sinners with indescribable brilliancy throughout the Holy City of God; they themselves are now radiant with His glory. Now they praise the Sacred Heart of Jesus as the pledge of eternal life, sanctity and bliss; now they are forever in the real presence of the glorified Saviour and the great desire of Jesus is accomplished: "I in them and Thou in Me; that they may be made perfect in one" (John 17:23).

My soul, do you not feel a burning desire for such glory and bliss? Then offer yourself to the divine Heart of Jesus and unite yourself with Him by true love and the imitation of His virtues. Do not believe, however, that you can become a perfect saint this very day; no, today you are but beginning. But continue your good efforts tomorrow, the day after and every day. Once you are one with Jesus through sanctifying grace, you will find it easier to avoid sin; and if you do not cease to look to Jesus for help, you will become stronger and more perfect from day to day, and His love will make perfect His work of salvation.

DEVOTION FOR COMMUNION

The assurance of being one with our Saviour and the hope of seeing the glory of the Sacred Heart of Jesus in eternity is indeed sufficient reward for the efforts and sacrifices which are required for frequent Holy Communion.

BEFORE HOLY COMMUNION

Faith
Jesus, my Lord and my God, with the same reverence with which the Apostles at the Last Supper heard Thy amazing words, ". . . eat ye all of this, this is My Body," I now approach Thy altar, because I firmly believe that the priest, to whom Thou hast given Thy divine power, pronounces in Thy name the words of consecration: "This is My Body." Thy word, O Jesus, is truth.

The words which Thou didst pronounce at the Last Supper have not lost their efficacy. I firmly believe that today Thou wilt change bread into Thy Flesh and wine into Thy Blood; and because Thy Body is not dead, but alive and glorified and Thy Blood is not cold and lifeless, but united with Thy living Body, therefore I believe that at the Consecration Thou wilt descend upon the altar truly living, as God and as man. And then Thou wilt become Food for my soul. I shall receive Thee on my tongue and into my heart. Thou wilt be in me, and I shall live entirely in Thee. Thou art the vine, and I am the branch; even as the branch cannot live when separated from the vine, so I cannot live without Thee. Thou art the way, the truth and the life; no one can come to the Father except through Thee. O Jesus, strengthen my faith in Thy holy presence and in the efficacy of the Holy Communion which I am about to receive.

Hope

O most merciful Jesus, Thou didst set a limit neither to the greatness of Thy sacrifice nor to the depths of Thy humiliations, in order to grant a place of refuge within Thy Heart for those who desire to renounce the world and to follow Thee. Therefore I hope that I, too, am numbered among those happy souls whom Thou didst so lovingly remember in Thy last priestly prayer; for Thou didst pray not only for the Apostles, but also for those who, through their teaching, would believe in Thee. Behold, I believe all things whatsoever Thy holy Catholic Church teaches. I humbly submit to all her rules and commandments because Thou hast bestowed Thy divine assistance and power upon her and didst pray for her. I may therefore confidently hope to share in the fruits of salvation which she brings forth because she receives her life from Thee, the true vine.

My hope becomes more joyous and confident when I consider that Thou didst institute this Blessed Sacrament of the Altar in order to give Thyself as Food to the faithful, to unite Thyself intimately with them, to strengthen them in virtue and to give them an unfailing pledge of eternal life. I am confident that after this Holy Communion Thou wilt pray: "I will that where I am, they also whom Thou hast given Me may be with Me; that they may see My glory" (John 17: 24). Behold, I place all my trust in the salutary effects of this Holy Communion, and I confidently hope for eternal salvation.

Love and Contrition

O most Sacred Heart of Jesus, fountain of life and holiness, model of all virtues, reflection of the glory of God, I hasten to Thee to engulf my miserable heart in Thy glory, to enkindle it with Thy love and to animate and sanctify it anew through Thy divine grace. Heart of Jesus, full of love for me, inflame my heart with love of Thee; grant that I may love only what Thou lovest, and hate and detest whatsoever is displeasing to Thee.

Alas, had I only known Thee before as I know Thee now! How sorry and mortified I am when I see the sins of my past life, the places where I have sinned, perhaps alone, with only Thee as a witness of my disobedience against Thy holy will, the persons who, through my fault, have been injured in soul or body. Still more am I put to shame by the remembrance of the many proofs of Thy love, the many confessions and Holy Communions which, alas, remained without fruit because I lacked the necessary love and faith. Henceforth, O Jesus, I shall hate sin above all things and shall love Thee, my only good, with all my heart. O Jesus, this is my intention and solemn promise. Help me with Thy grace to remain faithful.

Prayer to the Saints

All you saints of God, who stand before the throne of the Lamb, vested in white garments and bearing palms in your hands, permeated with the glory of the Sacred Heart of Jesus, wrapt in a sea of bliss and ecstasy . . . how blessed you are to have reached your eternal throne. You have gone before me, have shown the way which leads to the Marriage Feast of the Lamb; you have fought the good fight and can now rest forever. Blessed are you who were poor in spirit, because now you enjoy the inexhaustible riches of the glory of God; blessed are you who have preserved your hearts pure in the mire of this sinful world, because now you see the beauty of God; blessed are you who wept in sorrow for the sins of the world, because now the tears have vanished from your eyes and all your longing has been satisfied; blessed are you who have "suffered persecution for justice' sake," because yours is the kingdom of heaven. I beg you to tell me where you received the strength to dedicate your lives wholly to the service of God, to sanctify yourselves amidst the temptations of the world, to steel your hearts against the onslaughts of the flesh, sensuality, pride and avarice. You blessed Apostles and martyrs, you holy bishops and confessors, youths and virgins, from what inexhaustible fountain did you obtain the grace of perseverance? Was it not from the Heart of Jesus in the Blessed Sacrament? Yes, with the Saviour in your hearts it was easy to despise the world, to overcome temptations, to carry the cross of suffering and trails and to follow Him.

Oh, help me from your thrones in heaven through your powerful intercession with the Heart of Jesus, and obtain for me the grace to receive this Holy Communion so worthily that it may unite me forever with my God and Redeemer, and that hereafter, in union with you, I may praise eternally the mercy of God; that all may be one, as He and the Father are one; one in the beatific vision of his glory. Amen.

Desire

O Jesus, glory of the saints and of all souls that fear God, come and sanctify me. My soul longs for the precious stream of grace which flows from Thy Heart, the fountain of life and holiness. O my Jesus, I believe in Thee, I hope and trust in Thee, I love Thee with a burning desire to possess Thee forever. Again I most humbly confess my faults, my most grievous faults. O Jesus, be merciful to me, a poor sinner. Amen.

"Eucharistic Heart of Jesus, have mercy on us." *Indulgence: 300 days.*

AFTER HOLY COMMUNION

The month of November is especially dedicated to the memory of the poor souls in purgatory. Therefore do not neglect to pray for them today with special fervor and to recommend them to the merciful Heart of Jesus. Perhaps they hope to receive relief from their pains and admission to the Wedding Feast of the Lamb through your Holy Communion today. Listen with love and compassion as they call upon you from the depths of their prison: "Have pity on me, have pity on me, at least you my friends" (Job 19).

Salutation

O most Sacred Heart of my Saviour, now so intimately united with me, I salute and welcome Thee with a joyous heart. At last Thou art all mine and I am all Thine, I cling to Thee with all the love of my heart. Tell me what I must do to glorify Thee and to save my soul, and then grant me the grace to do Thy holy will. Thou art the vine; I am only the branch; I can bear fruit only as long as I am one with Thee. Behold, I am prepared to hearken to Thy voice and to live according to Thy holy will. Do with me what Thou wilt, I am Thine forever.

Thanksgiving

O most loving and merciful God, I owe Thee everlasting gratitude because Thou, the King of kings and Lord of hosts, didst come to me this day, and through this holy Sacrament didst become one with me. How can I ever thank Thee for this great honor? How can I repay Thee for this favor? How is it possible for a poor creature to give adequate thanks for this gift? In this holy mystery Thou didst permit us to share not only in Thy divinity, but also in Thy sacred humanity and in all its merits. Thou didst give us Thy Flesh and Blood, together with all the treasures and merits which Thou didst gain through them. O wonderful, incomprehensible gift, which the world does not understand, but which is worthy of eternal hymns of praise. O Jesus, divine Restorer of our souls, it is impossible for Thee to grant other riches comparable to these. Thou didst speak words of truth and love when Thou didst say to Thy Father: "For them do I sanctify myself, that they also may be sanctified in truth" (John 17:19). Thou dost sanctify Thyself, and I receive the fruits of Thy sanctification; Thou performest the deeds, and I receive the reward; Thou art poor, and I become rich; Thou dost receive the punishment, and I obtain the pardon; the last drop of Thy Blood is demanded, and to me are given health and life. These pains which Thou didst endure, these lashes, these thorns, these nails and this Precious Blood have appeased the justice of Thy Father. Thy tears have washed away my sins, Thy wounds have healed me, and Thy scourging, which tore Thy sacred Flesh, has paid my debt of sin. O blessed happiness for those who have entered into this wonderful communion with God, because through it they have received infinite treasures. And what did we give that we should receive so much? It is solely the effect of Thy grace and Thy love. The sun gives light, fire causes heat, water refreshes, because nature bestows these powers on them; and it is according to Thy nature, O God, to be merciful and to pardon; but it is most incomprehensible that, whilst Thou hast mercy on us, Thou art severe with Thyself. Thy nature is goodness, infinite goodness; and it is part of this goodness to give it freely to others. Thou hast given us Thy very Self. Thou wast born into this world to be our Brother; Thou didst suffer death that we might obtain life; Thou dost rule in heaven to be our reward, and Thou dost give Thyself to us as Food for our souls that we may become worthy of this reward.

How, then, can I thank Thee adequately, O Lord, if my gratitude is to be measured by the greatness of Thy favors? I read in Holy Scripture that Moses was commanded to place a golden vase filled with manna into the Ark of the Covenant so that future generations would know what kind of bread their forefathers had eaten during the forty years in the desert. If this material bread was to be preserved in such a sacred place, as a perpetual remembrance to the chosen people, how highly must we not esteem the imperishable Food which bestows eternal life upon those who receive it worthily? Man is too insignificant to give Thee adequate thanks for this gift. In my inability to manifest a gratitude worthy of Thy grace I take refuge in Thee, and with the Prophet I say: 'I will take the chalice of salvation and I will call upon the name of the Lord" (Ps. 115:4).

Therefore I beg of Thee, O Lord, to accept this holy Sacrament as a thanksgiving for all Thy favors, as atonement for my sins, and as a plea for strength to amend my life. May I always detest whatever is displeasing to Thee. Through the Sacrament of Thy Flesh and Blood and in honor of Thy holy name help me to cling to Thee henceforth, to love Thee and to live in union with Thee forever. Be merciful to all sinners; bring back into Thy Church all those who have been led astray by heresy or schism; enlighten the faithful that they may know Thee better, and strengthen all who are burdened with cares and labor. Come to the assistance of those for whom I am in duty bound to pray; comfort those to whom, next to Thee, I owe my life and so many favors: my parents, benefactors and friends. Have mercy on all those for whom Thou didst shed Thy precious Blood;

pardon the living and grant them Thy grace; grant eternal rest and joy to the departed.

O my Lord and my God, with joyous heart I consecrate myself entirely to Thee. In all things I submit to Thy holy will, which I honor and adore with greatest reverence. It is my earnest desire that Thy most wise, most just and adorable intentions and commandments be fulfilled in me. Through Thy infinite goodness grant me the grace to accomplish whatsoever Thou desirest in my behalf for time and eternity. Amen.

Act of Consecration

My most beloved Jesus, today I consecrate myself again without reserve to Thy divine Heart. I consecrate to Thee my body with all its senses and my soul with all its faculties. I consecrate to Thee all my thoughts, words and actions, all my sufferings and labors, all my hopes and all my joys; and, above all, I consecrate to Thee my poor heart, in order that it may love only Thee and may be consumed as a victim in the fire of Thy love. Accept, O Jesus, my most sweet Spouse, my ardent desire to console Thy divine Heart and to be Thine forever. Take possession of me in such a manner that henceforth I may have no other liberty than that of loving Thee, no other life than that of suffering and dying for Thee. I place unlimited trust in Thee, and from Thy infinite mercy I hope for the pardon of my sins. I place into Thy hands all my cares, especially that of my eternal salvation. I promise to love Thee and to honor Thee until the last moment of my life, and to propagate as much as I am able the devotion to Thy Sacred Heart. Dispose of me, O my Jesus, according to Thy good pleasure. I seek no other reward than Thy greater glory and Thy holy love. Grant me the grace to set up my dwelling-place in Thy divine Heart, where I desire to pass every day of my life, where I desire to breathe my last breath. Set up in my heart Thy abode, the chosen spot for Thy repose, so that we may remain ever closely united until one day I shall be able to praise, love and possess Thee for all eternity in heaven, where I will sing forever the infinite mercies of Thy most Sacred Heart.

Prayer for the Poor Souls

O Jesus, Redeemer of the world, be our salvation. Holy

Virgin Mary, Mother of God, pray for us. We humbly and earnestly beg of Thee to keep us from all evil and to enrich us with every grace. O Jesus, I salute, adore and praise Thee, and I give thanks for all the graces and favors which Thou didst bestow upon Thy holy Mother and all Thy elect. I join the saints in the gratitude and praise which they offer Thee for the assistance they received through Thy incarnation, passion and death. I beg of Thee, through the intercession of Thy glorious Mother and all the saints, to be gracious to the poor souls for whom I pray. Eternal rest grant unto them, O Lord, and let the perpetual light shine upon them. May they rest in peace. Amen.

FIRST FRIDAY IN DECEMBER

Heart of Jesus, King and center of all hearts, have mercy on us.

"All power is given to Me in heaven and on earth." (Matt. 28:18)

Meditation

Jesus was a descendant of King David and therefore had a right to the royal throne of Judea. However, Jesus did not desire to be an earthly king, but despised all worldly honors. He chose the cross for a throne, a wreath of thorns for a crown, a fool's garment for the regal purple and a reed for His scepter. When Pilate asked Him: "Art Thou the King of the Jews?" Jesus answered: "Thou sayest it. My kingdom is not of this world." Pilate therefore said to Him: "Art Thou a king, then?" Jesus answered: "Thou sayest that I am a king. For this was I born, and for this I came into the world; that I should give testimony to the truth. Everyone that is of the truth, heareth My voice" (John 18:37).

Christian soul, you understand that the kingdom in which our Redeemer desires to rule is the spiritual kingdom of truth, the kingdom of men's hearts. He does not desire to be the leader of great armies, but the king of the hearts of those who believe and hope in Him.

We know that after His resurrection, immediately before His ascension into heaven, Jesus exercised the Messianic power of His kingship. He gathered His Apostles about Him and spoke to them: "All power is given to Me in heaven, and on earth." What a majestic word! Did any king or emperor ever speak thus? Certainly not, because he would have been ridiculed. But Jesus spoke these words solemnly and emphatically, and the world bows before this word of its King. He is, indeed, King of the entire world, the King of all men; not only of those who believe in Him, but also of all nations, races and tribes; and because He does not desire so much to rule the bodies of men, but rather their hearts and souls, He is without doubt the King of all hearts.

Consider now, that the King of hearts commands: "Going, therefore, teach ye all nations; baptizing them in the name of the Father, and of the Son, and of the Holy Ghost. Teaching them to observe all things whatsoever I have commanded you" (Matt. 28:19-20). It is His sovereign will, therefore, that through Baptism all mankind be received into His kingdom and through faith and good works become its loyal citizens. How wonderful it would be if every human being, without exception, would heed the call of the diving Heart of Jesus to enter into His kingdom, the Church, and to imitate His life of virtue. It would be heaven on earth for them. The kings of this world would then need neither soldiers nor cannons, because all nations would be of one heart and one soul, and the undisputed King of all hearts would be the most loving Heart of Jesus. Through meekness and mercy He would conquer all hearts. But alas, conditions as they now exist do not correspond to the glorious ideal of the Heart of Jesus. Nevertheless, the divine Heart is truly the King and center of all hearts. It is not the fault of the sun that many are blind and do not see its light; neither is it the fault of the King of glory, the Heart of Jesus, that so many are spiritually blind and do not recognize His glory. And yet He is in our very midst according to His own words: "Behold I am with you all days, even to the consummation of the world" (Matt. 28:20). We find great comfort in the thought that in the Holy City of God the Heart of Jesus will reign over the hearts of the elect forever and ever.

Until that blessed time arrives, all His subjects, and you, too, must faithfully perform the sacred duty of living as an apostle of His Heart and assisting in the growth of His kingdom. It would not be a sign of great love on your part if, in spite of the indifference and insults heaped upon your divine King, you would still remain cold and uninterested. About the end of the last century the supreme shepherd of the Church, the Vicar of Jesus Christ, exhorted the faithful to consecrate themselves without reserve to the Sacred Heart of Jesus and to do this not only for themselves, but also for those who do not know and therefore cannot love this kingly Heart.

Christian soul, consecrate yourself again and again, and by your devout prayers and exemplary life, by your love and kindness, accomplish the will of the Holy Father, namely, that Christ, the Lord and King, be known, loved and adored by all people. May the Sacred Heart of Jesus be loved everywhere. O Heart of Jesus, King and center of all hearts, have mercy on us.

BEFORE HOLY COMMUNION

Adoration

O eternal King, who hast erected Thy throne in the tabernacle in order to live among Thy people to the end of time, I adore thee in profound reverence. I firmly believe in Thy kingly power and that this power is Thine by right of Thy divinity. Thou dost possess this divine power from all eternity because Thou art the Son of the eternal Father. Thou hast merited this infinite power by Thy divine and sublime life, Thy humility and meekness, Thy obedience and love, by Thy miracles and prophecies, Thy terrible sufferings and voluntary sacrifice on the cross. Thou dost constantly merit our belief in Thy divine power by the graces which Thou dost shower upon the hearts of men for their temporal and eternal welfare, by Thy Flesh and Blood in the Blessed Sacrament, and by the full surrender of Thy most loving Heart to all who are faithful to Thee. Hosanna to the Son of God! Hosanna to the Son of David! Blessed is He that cometh in the name of the Lord!

Faith, Humility, Contrition

My God and my King, I believe that Thou art really and truly present in the Blessed Sacrament to rule as the King of all hearts. From Thy throne in the tabernacle, Thou dost invite us in these words: "Come to Me, all you that labor, and are burdened, and I will refresh you" (Matt. 11:28). Thou art the King of kings; Thou didst come into the world and didst institute this Blessed Sacrament in order that men might always and everywhere adore Thee as their King. Behold, I believe firmly and unswervingly in Thy kingly power, and surrender myself to it in complete humility.

I abhor and detest sin because by sin Thy regal majesty is insulted and trodden under foot. In shame and in deepest sorrow I must confess that through my sins I, too, joined those who cried out: "We have no king but Caesar."

My dearest Jesus, most gracious King, here and now I denounce my shameful behavior and solemnly declare that I gratefully acknowledge Thy kingly rule over me and all creatures. Yes, rule over my body and soul, over my intellect and will, but above all be Thou the supreme Ruler within my heart. Enter Thou into my heart and cast out of it all worldly thoughts and desires, all inordinate inclinations and all attachment to temporal things. Sanctify my heart, adorn it with the wealth of Thy graces. Be unto me a benign and merciful King. Amen.

"Jesus, Son of David, have mercy on me." *Indulgence: 500 days. Plenary once a month.*

"Sacred Heart of Jesus, Thy Kingdom come." *Indulgence: 300 days. Plenary once a month.*

Love

Immortal and eternal King of glory, the hosts of heaven bow down before Thee; the choirs of angels rejoice while they sing: "Holy, holy holy, the Lord God of hosts; all the earth is full of His glory" (Is. 6:3). The cherubim and seraphim are inflamed with love for Thee, and are so wrapt with ecstasy in the light of Thy glory as to be compelled to veil their faces before Thee, being unable to endure the splendor of Thy majesty. Oh, could I but love Thee as they do! O glorious Heart of the eternal King, inflame my heart with Thy divine love. Although I cannot see Thee in Thy glory, nevertheless Thy real presence in the Blessed Sacrament is the clearest proof of Thy love. I no longer doubt that Thou lovest me with the same love which inflames and delights the millions of saints and angels in heaven. Deign to accept this most sincere pledge of my love for Thee: O loving Heart of my King. I love Thee; I love Thee now and will love Thee forever and ever. Amen.

Desire

O Jesus, meek and humble King of all hearts, I await Thy coming with great joy. Could I but receive Thee as Thy beloved disciples and friends have received Thee: as my King, yes, as the King of all hearts! I have no greater desire than that Thou shouldst enter into my heart to rule forever. Come, Emmanuel, Heart of hearts, come and take possession of what is Thine. Do with me what Thou wilt. Come and enrich me with the wealth of Thy grace; come and ennoble my soul, pervade it with Thy glory and preserve it forever from the hands of Thy enemies. Amen.

"Jesus, for Thee I live; Jesus, for Thee I die; Jesus, I am Thine in life and in death. Amen." *Indulgence: 100 days. Plenary once a month.*

AFTER HOLY COMMUNION

Thanksgiving

O King of hearts, Thou art really and truly present within my heart. Thy divine Majesty has humbled Itself and has sought the lowliest dwelling-place to be found on earth. Oh, what honor has been bestowed upon me! How thankful should I be to Thee! O exalted King and God, I cannot thank Thee in any better way than by adoring Thy infinite Majesty and submitting myself entirely to Thy holy will. Accept supreme command within me and fill this poor abode which Thou has chosen with the beauty and riches of Thy divine Heart. Inflame my heart, inflame my soul, that they may burn with ardent love for Thee. O Jesus, my Lord and my God, henceforth I with to be entirely Thine. I consecrate myself to Thee; I offer Thee my body and my soul and all their faculties, my thoughts and desires, all my words and deeds; all for Thy greater honor and glory.

With all my heart I desire that Thou be known, loved and adored by all as the King of hearts. I most earnestly wish that I could make due reparation for all the disrespect and the offenses which are heaped upon Thy divine Heart, and for all the insults and blasphemies which rise daily from a sinful world to Thy throne of love and grace. Would that my reverent Hosanna could be heard above the diabolical clamor of Thy enemies, who curse Thy authority and with the Jews of old call out in protest: "We have no king but Caesar." As a reparation for all these insults I, who am so poor and sinful, offer Thee the Immaculate Heart of Mary, the glorious Queen of Heaven, together with the love of the angels and all the merits of the saints. O ye saints of heaven, and especially thou, O Queen of the Universe, permit me to join you in your glorious song of praise to the King of hearts: "Holy, holy, holy, the Lord of hosts, all the earth is full of His glory."

Divine Heart of Jesus, trusting in Thy infinite power and goodness, I come to Thee as a subject comes to his king and as a servant to his master. I trustingly place my petitions before

Thee, O Jesus, because Thou didst deign to descend from Thy heavenly throne in order to take up Thy abode in my heart. Behold, I am so poor and weak that I can do nothing without Thy grace. So often have I made good resolutions to lead a better life, to become humble, patient, meek, obedient, devout in my prayers, zealous in the fulfillment of my duties, and to deny myself; and yet I have repeatedly fallen into the same sins. I conjure Thee to grant me today the grace to make and earnest and lasting resolution. Do not permit me to forget Thy loving visit, nor ever to become lukewarm in Thy service. Inflame my heart with the fire of Thy love; encourage me to live a truly Christian life, and through Thy indefatigable love grant that I may never weary in my zeal for Thy greater honor and glory. Behold, I am resolved henceforth to assist in the propagation of Thy Kingdom on earth. In word and deed I shall endeavor to teach those about me to know and to love Thee. By assisting the foreign mission I shall try to the best of my ability to draw pagans, who still live in the shadow of spiritual death, to the knowledge of Thy infinite glory. O divine Heart of Jesus, increase the number of Thy missionary servants; reveal Thyself to all as the loving King of hearts, and through the sweet power of Thy love constrain them to serve Thee and to render homage to Thee alone. Amen.

"Sacred Heart of Jesus, Thy Kingdom come." *Indulgence: 300 days.*

"O Lord, increase in us the Faith." *Indulgence: 500 days. Plenary once a month.*

Prayer to St. Francis de Sales

O my Jesus, Thy Heart is the benevolent Heart of peace and grace. Thy Heart is also a magnificent temple, in which Thou desirest us to live. I have a most ardent desire to choose this soul-inspiring Heart as the King of all hearts. I beg of Thee to lead at least the efforts and desires of my own heart to one purpose, namely, to beg for nothing else but that Thou be its King forever.

O my Jesus, take complete possession of my heart and be Thou the King of this insignificant but truly submissive kingdom. May Thy Heart ever live in mine, and may the will of Thy Heart always rule and guide the will of my heart. Yes, may

Thy precious Blood flow uninterruptedly through its veins. O Jesus, I will ever raise my heart to Thine, which alone is worthy of all love. My heart shall constantly meditate upon Thee, adore Thee and praise Thy holy will. May Thy Heart ever dispose of me according to Thy holy will; I desire to be Thine now and for all eternity.

O my Jesus, I beg of Thee to accept my heart and to give me Thine instead, so that I may live only in Thy love. In the future, grant that I may so guide my heart that it may always live and labor according to the desires of Thy Heart. I, too, shall then please Thee by being holy, meek and humble during all my life, because the path of holiness, love and humility is the one most cherished by Thy Heart, O my divine Saviour. Amen.

Part III: Devotions and Indulgenced Prayers

PRAYERS FOR FIRST FRIDAYS

Litany of the Sacred Heart

Lord, have mercy on us.
Christ, have mercy on us.
Lord, have mercy on us.
Christ, hear us.
Christ, graciously hear us.
God the Father of heaven, * have mercy on us.
God the Son, Redeemer of the world, *
God the Holy Ghost, *
Holy Trinity, one God, *
Heart of Jesus, Son of the eternal Father, *
Heart of Jesus, formed by the Holy Ghost in the womb of the
Virgin Mother, *
Heart of Jesus, substantially united to the Word of God, *
Heart of Jesus, of infinite majesty, *
Heart of Jesus, sacred temple of God, *
Heart of Jesus, tabernacle of the Most High, *
Heart of Jesus, house of God and gate of heaven, *
Heart of Jesus, burning furnace of charity, *
Heart of Jesus, abode of Justice and love, *
Heart of Jesus, full of goodness and love, *
Heart of Jesus, abyss of all virtues, *
Heart of Jesus, most worthy of all praise, *
Heart of Jesus, king and center of all hearts, *
Heart of Jesus, in whom are all the treasures of wisdom and
knowledge, *
Heart of Jesus, in whom dwells the fullness of divinity, *
Heart of Jesus, in whom the Father was well pleased, *
Heart of Jesus, of whose fullness we have all received, *
Heart of Jesus, desire of the everlasting hills, *
Heart of Jesus, patient and most merciful, *
Heart of Jesus, enriching all who invoke Thee, *
Heart of Jesus, fountain of life and holiness, *

Heart of Jesus, propitiation for our sins, *
Heart of Jesus, loaded down with opprobrium, *
Heart of Jesus, bruised for our offenses, *
Heart of Jesus, obedient unto death, *
Heart of Jesus, pierced with a lance, *
Heart of Jesus, source of all consolation, *
Heart of Jesus, our life and resurrection, *
Heart of Jesus, our peace and reconciliation, *
Heart of Jesus, victim for our sins, *
Heart of Jesus, salvation of those who hope in Thee, *
Heart of Jesus, hope of those who die in Thee, *
Heart of Jesus, delight of all the saints, *
Lamb of God, who takest away the sins of the world, spare us, O Lord.
Lamb of God, who takest away the sins of the world, graciously hear us, O Lord.
Lamb of God, who takest away the sins of the world, have mercy on us.

V. Jesus, meek and humble of heart,
R. Make our hearts like unto Thine.

Let us pray.
O almighty and eternal God, look upon the Heart of Thy dearly beloved Son, and upon the praise and satisfaction He offers Thee in the name of sinners. Be Thou appeased, and grant pardon to those who seek Thy mercy, in the name of the same Jesus Christ, Thy Son, who liveth and reigneth with Thee, in the unity of the Holy Ghost, world without end. Amen.
Indulgence: 7 years. Plenary once a month. Must be said with the versicle and oration.

Act of Reparation to the Sacred Heart of Jesus
to be said on the Feast of the Sacred Heart
O sweet Jesus, whose overflowing charity for men is requited by so much forgetfulness, negligence and contempt, behold us prostrate before Thy altar, eager to repair by a special act of homage the cruel indifference and the injuries to which Thy loving Heart is everywhere subject.

Mindful, alas, that we ourselves have had a share in such great indignities, which we now deplore from the depths of our hearts, we humbly ask Thy pardon and declare our readiness to atone by voluntary expiation, not only for our own personal offenses, but also for the sins of those who, straying from the path of salvation, refuse in their obstinate infidelity to follow Thee, their Shepherd and Leader, or, renouncing the vows of their Baptism, have cast off the sweet yoke of Thy law.

We are now resolved to expiate each and every deplorable outrage committed against Thee; we are determined to make amends for the manifold offenses against Christian modesty in unbecoming dress and behavior, for all the foul seductions laid to ensnare the feet of the innocent, for the frequent violation of Sundays and holy days, and the shocking blasphemies uttered against Thee and Thy saints. We wish also to make amends for the insults to which Thy Vicar on earth and Thy priests are subjected, for the profanation, by conscious neglect or terrible acts of sacrilege, of the very Sacrament of Thy Divine love; and lastly for the public crimes of nations, who resist the rights and the teaching authority of the Church which Thou hast founded.

Would, O Divine Jesus, we were able to wash away such abominations with our blood! We now offer, in reparation for these violations of Thy honor, the satisfaction which Thou didst once make to Thy eternal Father on the Cross, and which Thou dost continue to renew daily on our altars. We offer it in union with the acts of atonement of Thy Virgin Mother and all the saints, and of the pious faithful on earth.

We sincerely promise to make recompense, as far as we can, with the help of Thy grace, for all neglect of Thy great love, and for the sins we and others have committed in the past. Henceforth we will live a life of unwavering faith, of purity of conduct, and of perfect observance of the precepts of the Gospel, especially that of charity. We promise to the best of our power to prevent others from offending Thee, and to bring as many as possible to follow Thee.

O loving Jesus, through the intercession of the Blessed Virgin Mary, our model in reparation, deign to receive the voluntary offering we make of this act of expiation, and by the crowning gift of perseverance keep us faithful unto death in our duty and the allegiance we owe to Thee, so that we may one day come to that happy home, where Thou with the Father and the Holy Ghost, livest and reignest, God, world without end. Amen.

Indulgences: Seven years on the Feast of the Sacred Heart for all present at the recitation of this Act and of the Litany of the Sacred Heart before the Blessed Sacrament exposed in any church or oratory. All who are thus present may gain a Plenary Indulgence if they go to Confession and Communion.

Consecration of the Human Race to the Sacred Heart of Jesus
on the Feast of Christ the King
(ordered by His Holiness Pope Pius XI)

Most Sweet Jesus, Redeemer of the human race, look down upon us humbly prostrate before Thy altar. We are Thine, and Thine we wish to be; but, to be more surely united with Thee, behold, each one of us freely consecrates himself today to Thy most Sacred Heart. Many, indeed, have never known Thee; many, too, despising Thy precepts, have rejected Thee. Have mercy on them all, most merciful Jesus, and draw them to Thy Sacred Heart. Be Thou King, O Lord, not only of the faithful who have never forsaken Thee, but also of the prodigal children who have abandoned Thee; grant that they may quickly return to their Father's house, lest they die of wretchness and hunger. Be Thou King of those who are deceived by erroneous opinions, or whom discord keeps aloof, and call them back to the harbor of truth and unity of faith, so that soon there may be but one flock and one Shepherd.

Be Thou King of all those who are still involved in the darkness of idolatry or Islamism, and refuse not to draw them all into the light and kingdom of God. Turn Thine eyes of mercy toward the children of that race, once Thy chosen people; of old they called down upon themselves the Blood of the Saviour; may it now descend upon them a laver of redemption and of life.

Grant, O Lord, to Thy Church assurance of freedom and immunity from harm; give peace and order to all nations, and make the earth resound from pole to pole with one cry: Praise to the divine Heart that wrought our salvation; to It be honor and glory forever. Amen.

Act of Consecration by St. Margaret Mary

I, N.N., give and consecrate to the Sacred Heart of our Lord

Jesus Christ my person and my life, my actions, penances and sufferings. I do not wish to make use of any part of my being for the future except in honoring, loving and glorifying that Sacred Heart.

It is my irrevocable will to be entirely His, and to do everything for His love. I renounce with my whole heart whatever might displease Him.

I take Thee, then, O most Sacred Heart, as the sole object of my love, as the protector of my life, the pledge of my salvation, the remedy of my frailty and my inconstancy, the repairer of all the defects of my life, and my secure refuge in the hour of death.

Be, then, O Heart of goodness, my justification before God the Father, and remove from me the thunderbolts of His just wrath. O Heart of love, I place my whole confidence in Thee. While I fear all things from my malice and frailty, I hope all things from Thy goodness.

Consume, then, in me whatever can displease Thee or be opposed to Thee. May Thy pure love be so deeply impressed upon my heart that it will be forever impossible for me to be separated from Thee, or forget Thee.

I implore Thee by all Thy goodness, that my name may be written in Thee, for in Thee I wish to place all my happiness and all my glory, living and dying in very bondage to Thee. Amen.

Indulgence: 3 years. Plenary once a month.

Daily Act of Oblation

O Lord Jesus Christ, in union with that divine intention wherewith Thou didst on earth offer praises to God through Thy Sacred Heart, and now dost continue to offer them in all places in the Sacrament of the Eucharist, and wilt do so to the end of the world, I most willingly offer Thee, throughout this entire day without the smallest exception, all my intentions and thoughts, all my affections and desires, all my words and actions, that they may be conformed to the most Sacred Heart of the Blessed Virgin Mary, ever Immaculate.

Indulgence: 3 years once a day. Plenary once a month.

Memorare to the Sacred Heart

Remember, O most sweet Jesus, that never has it been heard that anyone who had recourse to Thy Sacred Heart, invoked Its protection, or implored Its mercy, was left unaided. Inspired by this confidence, I hasten to Thee, and bewailing my offenses, I stand before Thee. Do not despise my prayers, O Sacred Heart of Jesus, but graciously hear and grant them. Amen.

Preparation for a Happy Death

Having cleansed and strengthened your soul at the fountain of all sanctity, you will derive much benefit by closing the First Friday with an earnest preparation for death. Draw a mental picture of your own death, as if you were to die this very hour, and declare yourself prepared to do everything that you would then consider necessary, or at least profitable. Ask yourself: Am I ready to die? Answer this question honestly, as you understand the condition of your soul. Then recite the following:

Prayer for a Happy Death

O Lord Jesus, God of goodness and Father of mercies, I draw nigh to Thee with a contrite and humble heart; to Thee I recommend the last hour of my life, and that judgment which awaits me afterwards.

When my feet, benumbed with death, shall admonish me that my course in this life is drawing to an end: merciful Jesus, have mercy on me.

When my hands, cold and trembling, shall no longer be able to clasp the crucifix, and, against my will, shall let it fall upon my bed of suffering: merciful Jesus, have mercy on me.

When my eyes, dim and troubled at the approach of death, shall fix themselves on Thee, my last and only support: merciful Jesus, have mercy on me.

When my lips, cold and trembling, pronounce for the last time Thy adorable name: merciful Jesus, have mercy on me.

When my face, pale and livid, shall inspire the beholders with pity and dismay; when my hair, bathed in the sweat of death and stiffening on my head, shall forebode my approaching end: merciful Jesus, have mercy on me.

When my ears, soon to be forever closed to the discourse of men, shall be open to that irrevocable decree which is to fix my doom for all eternity: merciful Jesus, have mercy on me.

When my imagination, agitated by dreadful specters, shall

sink into an abyss of anguish; when my soul, affrightened with the sight of my iniquities and the terrors of Thy judgment, shall have to struggle against the angels of darkness, who will endeavor to conceal Thy mercies from my eyes and plunge me into despair: merciful Jesus, have mercy on me.

When my poor heart, oppressed with suffering and exhausted by its continual struggles with the enemies of its salvation, shall feel the pangs of death: merciful Jesus, have mercy on me.

When the last tears, the sign of my approaching dissolution, shall drop from my eyes, receive them as a sacrifice of expiation for my sins; grant that I may expire a victim of penance, and then, in that dreadful moment: merciful Jesus, have mercy on me.

When my friends and relatives, encircling my bed, shall be moved with compassion for me and invoke Thy clemency in my behalf: merciful Jesus, have mercy on me.

When I shall lose the use of my senses, when the world vanishes from my sight, when I shall groan with anguish in my last agony and the pangs of death: merciful Jesus, have mercy on me.

When my last sighs shall compel my soul to issue from my body, accept them as born of a loving impatience to come to Thee: merciful Jesus, have mercy on me.

When my soul shall bid farewell to the world and leave my body lifeless, pale and cold, receive this separation as a homage which I willingly pay to Thy divine Majesty; and in that last moment of my mortal life: merciful Jesus, have mercy on me.

When at length my soul, admitted to Thy presence, shall first behold the immortal splendor of Thy Majesty, reject it not, but receive me into the loving embrace of Thy mercy, where I may forever sing Thy praises: merciful Jesus, have mercy on me.

Let us pray.

O God, who hast doomed all men to die, but has concealed from them the hour of their death, grant that I may pass my days in justice and holiness, and that I may be made worthy to leave this world in the embrace of Thy love, through the merits of our Lord Jesus Christ, who liveth and reigneth with Thee, in the unity of the Holy Ghost. Amen.

Recommendation to One's Guardian Angel for a Happy Hour of Death by St. Charles Borromeo

My good Angel: I know not when or how I shall die. It is possible I may be carried off suddenly, and that before my last sigh I may be deprived of all intelligence. Yet how many things I would wish to say to God on the threshold of eternity. In the full freedom of my will today, I come to charge you to speak for me at that fearful moment. You will say to Him, then, O my good Angel:

That I wish to die in the Roman Catholic Apostolic Church in which all the saints since Jesus Christ have died, and out of which there is no salvation.

That I ask the grace of sharing in the infinite merits of my Redeemer and that I desire to die in pressing to my lips the cross that was bathed in His Blood!

That I detest my sins because they displease Him, and that I pardon through love of Him all my enemies as I wish myself to be pardoned.

That I die willingly because He orders it and that I throw myself with confidence into His adorable Heart awaiting all His Mercy.

That in my inexpressible desire to go to Heaven I am disposed to suffer everything it may please His sovereign Justice to inflict on me.

That I love Him before all things, above all things and for His own sake; that I wish and hope to love Him with the Elect, His Angels and the Blessed Mother during all Eternity.
Do not refuse, O my Angel, to be my interpreter with God, and to protest to Him that these are my sentiments and my will. Amen.

Prayer of St. Alphonse Liguori, to be said at a Visit to the Blessed Sacrament

O my Lord Jesus Christ, who for the love which Thou bearest to men dost remain night and day in this Sacrament, full of tenderness and love, expecting, inviting and receiving all who come to visit Thee; I believe that Thou art present in the Sacrament of the Altar; I adore Thee in the depths of my own nothingness; and I thank Thee for all the graces which Thou hast granted me, especially for having vouchsafed to bestow Thyself upon me in this Sacrament, for having given me Thy own most holy Mother Mary for my advocate, and for having invited me to visit Thee in this church. I pay my homage this day to Thy adorable Heart, and I do so for the following three intentions: first, in thanksgiving for this great gift itself; secondly, in reparation for all the injuries which Thou hast received from all Thy enemies in this Sacrament; thirdly, by this visit I intend to adore Thee in all those places where Thou, sacramentally present, art least reverenced and most abandoned. My Jesus, I love Thee with my whole heart. I repent of having so many times heretofore displeased Thy infinite goodness. With the assistance of Thy grace I resolve never more to offend Thee; and at this present moment, poor sinner that I am, I consecrate myself wholly to Thee. I renounce my own will entirely and offer it to Thee together with my affections, my desires, and everything that I call my own. From this day forth do Thou with me, and with everything that belongs to me, whatever pleases Thee. I ask of Thee and desire only Thy holy love, final perseverance and the perfect fulfillment of Thy will. I commend to Thee the souls in purgatory, especially those who were most devoted to the Blessed Sacrament and to Mary most holy. Moreover, I commend to Thee all poor sinners. For this intention, O my dear Saviour Jesus, I unite all my affections with the affections of Thy most loving Heart; and thus united, I offer them to Thy Eternal Father, and I entreat Him in Thy name and for Thy love, to accept and answer them.

Indulgence: 5 years if said before the Blessed Sacrament. Plenary once a month.

DEVOTION FOR MASS

Eternal God, permit me to offer to Thee the Heart of Jesus Christ, Thy beloved Son, as He offers Himself to Thee. Deign to accept this gift from me together with all its desires, intentions and deeds. Because He offers Himself for me, and because I desire to agree with Him in all things, I beg of Thee to accept His sacrifice of Himself as entirely my own. Accept it so that I through His merits may receive all the graces of which I am in need, especially the grace of perseverance. Accept His intentions and desires as so many acts of love, adoration and praise, which I offer to Thy divine Majesty, because through Him only cast Thou be worthily honored and glorified. Amen.

Beginning of Mass

Praised and glorified forever be the most Sacred Heart of Jesus, which was pierced with a lance because of our sins. Praised be the Heart in which are hidden all the treasures of divine grace and love. In humility and with sincere sorrow for my sins I kneel before Thee, O God of my heart, and place within Thy Heart the confession of my guilt. Have mercy on me, a poor sinner, and pardon my sins by the sacred water and precious Blood which flowed from Thy pierced Heart. Most Sacred Heart of Jesus, have mercy on us.

At the Gloria

O my Jesus, incarnate Son of the heavenly Father, from Thy most Sacred Heart there flows into the hearts of the children of God the full measure of bliss, rest, joy, peace and every other blessing. Thy Sacred Heart is the fountain of all holiness, purity and perfection; Thy Heart is the seat of every virtue; Thy Heart is the delight of Thy Father, the joy of all the angels and saints; Thy most Sacred Heart is the altar on which are offered to the Blessed Trinity the most perfect sacrifices of praise, thanksgiving, and adoration. There is nothing in heaven nor on earth that is more beautiful, glorious, pure, sweet and blissful than Thy Heart; it is the object of the love, veneration and adoration of all the angels and saints and of all pure souls on earth. It is impossible to find words in which to pay adequate homage to Thy Sacred Heart; where can I find a language to express the feelings of my soul when I meditate upon Thy loving Heart, O Jesus? Behold, I kneel before Thee in profound reverence, adoring Thy most amiable Heart and offering to It, from the bottom of my heart, all praise and glory. Oh, could I but make reparation for all the sufferings which Thy loving Heart had to endure for our sake! Oh, could I but make reparation for all the pains which our sins have cause Thee. O my Jesus, design to accept this my desire. I know only too well that I am too miserable to make due reparation by my homage and adoration. Accept, instead, the praises of all pious souls, of all the saints in heaven, who love Thy divine Heart so fervently and in whom Thou dost find so much joy. I unite my desires with theirs, and in union with them I pray:

"May the Heart of Jesus in the most Blessed Sacrament be praised, adored and loved with grateful affection, at every moment, in all the tabernacles of the world, even to the end of time. Amen." (Indulgence 300 days.)

Epistle

O most Sacred Heart of Jesus, with what great longing did the prophets of old sigh for Thy advent! They longed for the Messiah, whose Heart was to be pierced with a lance and whose Blood was to give them assurance of their salvation. How often did they envy us, the future generations, who would be enabled to draw all grace from the cross of the Redeemer. The prophet Isaias wrote: "You shall draw waters with joy out of the Savior's fountains: and you shall say in that day: praise ye the Lord, and call upon His name: make His works known among the people: remember that His name is high. Sing ye to the Lord, for He hath done great things: shew this forth in all the earth. Rejoice, and praise, O thou habitation of Sion: for great is He that is in the midst of Thee, the Holy One of Israel (Is. 12:3-6).

Gospel

Most loving Savior Jesus Christ, with grateful reverence do I meditate upon the immeasurable love of Thy adorable Heart, which induced Thee to leave Thy peaceful home at Nazareth in order to preach the glorious message of salvation and to invite all nations to follow Thee: "Come to Me, all you that labor, and are burdened, and I will refresh you… and you shall find rest to your souls" (Matt. 11:28, 29). I thank Thee with all my heart for having called me to the true Faith, and I shall ever rejoice to profess my faith in Thee. Thou alone art the way, the truth and the life; whosoever believes in Thee and keeps Thy Commandments shall live forever.

Credo

Heart of Jesus, substantially united to the Word of God, Thou art the living fountain of all truth. I firmly believe in my heart and profess with my lips all that Thou, my Redeemer, hast taught and that Thy Church still teaches. I believe in God, the Father etc. (*Recite the Apostles' Creed*).

Offertory

O my Jesus, I kneel before Thee and entreat Thee to offer me on the altar as a sacrifice to Thy most amiable Heart. But because this my offering is worthy only of punishment, I beg of Thee, my divine Priest, to cleanse it, and to consume it as a perfect-burnt offering in the fire of Thy divine love, and to bestow upon me a new life of grace and of love for Thee. O Jesus, Thou only love of my heart, Thou sweet pain of my soul! I ask only one grace of Thee, namely, that I may live and die as a perpetual sacrifice to Thy most Sacred Heart, through a hatred of all things that displease Thee; as an offering to Thy Soul, that my own soul can endure; as an offering to Thy Body, by separating myself from all things that may please my body, and by a hatred of that sinful flesh which I desire to crucify for love of Thee. Amen.

Orate, Fratres

Heavenly Father, omnipotent God and Master, accept this offering from the hands of Thy priest, and grant him the grace and assistance of Thy Holy Spirit, so that he may worthily perform this holy and momentous act, which is so precious to the entire Church. May this holy Sacrifice redound to the greater glory of Thy Majesty, to an increase of joy to all the saints, to the benefit of Thy militant Church on earth, and to the consolation of the poor souls in purgatory.

Preface

I praise and glorify Thee, O most amiable Jesus, in union with that praise with which the Triune God praises Himself, with which Thou dost ever praise and glorify Him, and in which are united the Blessed Virgin Mary and all the angels and saints, who unceasingly sing the praises of Thy most glorious Majesty. I join my poor voice to theirs in thanksgiving for all the graces and blessings which Thou hast bestowed upon them and upon me, a poor sinner: Holy, holy, holy, Lord God of Sabaoth. Heaven and earth are full of Thy glory. Hosanna in the highest!

Blessed is He that cometh in the name of the Lord! Hosanna in the highest!

Before Consecration

O most gracious Jesus, I recommend to the solicitude of Thy love all those who have requested me to pray for them, because I know that this Thy love constrained Thee to come to this earth to save them and me. In union with the love with which Thou didst commend Thy spirit to the heavenly Father, I also recommend them to Thy most gracious Heart; I offer this Heart in union with that love with which at the Incarnation Thou didst offer It for our salvation and with which Thou didst so often give It to Thy faithful servants as a token of special friendship. By Thy love for me, I beg of Thee, grant Thy blessings to those for whom I pray and to those for whom I am in duty bound to pray.

Consecration

"Hail, saving Victim, offered on the gibbet of the cross for me and for the whole human race!"

"Hail, precious Blood, streaming from the wounds of my crucified Lord Jesus Christ, washing away the sins of the world!"

"Remember, O Lord, Thy servant, the work of Thy hands, whom Thou hast redeemed with Thy precious Blood!"

Indulgence: 500 days for each ejaculation, also when said separately, at the Elevation of the Mass.

After Consecration

O infinitely gracious Heart of my supreme love, it is impossible for me to love and glorify Thee with all the love with which Thou hast inflamed me; I call heaven and earth to my assistance and join the seraphim in their love for Thee. O Heart of Jesus, burning furnace of love! Thou dost inflame heaven and earth with this fire so that all creatures may breathe only Thy love. Grant that I may either suffer or die; at least convert my heart to such compelling love that it may consume itself entirely in the fire of Thy love. O divine fire, O purest flame of the Heart of my only love, burn me without mercy; consume me without clemency. May everything that can be called love, in heaven and on earth, enter my heart to dissolve me to ashes! O consuming fire of the Divinity, come and vanquish me! Burn and consume me in the flames of Thy pure love, which bestow eternal life upon those who die in them. Amen. (St. Margaret Mary Alacoque)

Memento for the Dead

O gracious Heart of my Redeemer, remember those helpless souls who died in Thy love, but who, on account of defects and faults, are not yet worthy to behold Thy glory. Relieve their terrible yearning, lessen their suffering and shorten their time of penance, through this Holy Sacrifice which Thou offerest to Thy heavenly Father.

Pater Noster

The profound reverence which Thou didst always manifest to Thy heavenly Father, and Thy earnest desire to restore His kingdom on earth and to lead all men to heaven, caused Thee, O most amiable Jesus, to teach us how to pray to the Father: Our Father, who art in heaven (etc.)

O merciful Lord and Saviour, arouse within my heart an earnest longing for the blessed mansion in heaven which Thou hast prepared for me. Permit me to partake of the precious Food of Thy holy Table, so that I may enjoy the sweet foretaste of the eternal joys of heaven. Deliver me from the evil of sin and grant me, instead, the peace of a good conscience. Amen.

Agnus Dei

Lamb of God, who takest away the sins of the world, have mercy on us.
Lamb of God, who takest away the sins of the world, have mercy on us.
Lamb of God, who takest away the sins of the world, grant us peace.

Lord Jesus Christ, who hast said to Thy Apostles: "Peace I leave with you, My peace I give unto you" (John 14:27), do not remember my sins, but look upon the faith of Thy Church and preserve her in peace and unity, who livest and reignest true God forever and ever. Amen.

Sweet Jesus, friend of mankind, Thou callest to us in the Blessed Sacrament: "Take ye and eat, this is My Body... Drink ye all of this, for this is My Blood" (Matt. 26). My heart longs for Thee because I believe in Thy Real Presence in the most Blessed Sacrament, and because I trust in the infinite goodness of Thy Heart. Oh, how gladly would I receive Thee in Holy Communion if I were only worthy of this grace! I implore Thee, through this Holy Mass to move my heart to real sorrow for my sins and a sincere love for Thee, that today I may receive Thee at least spiritually, and that soon I may receive Thee truly and really in Holy Communion. Create a clean heart within me, even as Thou dost to those who receive Thee worthily. Behold me, like the publican, striking my breast and saying: "Lord, be merciful to me a sinner."

O Lord, I am not worthy that Thou shouldst enter into my soul, but say only the word, and my soul shall be healed (*three times*).

After Communion

I praise Thee, almighty and omniscient Love; I extol Thee, O sweetest Love; I glorify Thee, O most amiable Love; in thanksgiving for all the blessings which Thy most sublime Divinity and sacred Humanity have bestowed upon us in the past and will grant us for all eternity through Thy most noble Heart. Amen.

Behold, O heavenly Father, our holy mother, the Church, has again offered the most sublime victim to Thee; that Victim which Thou didst send upon earth to be crucified for us. Accept it with that inexpressible love with which Thou didst welcome Thy beloved Son when He returned for this earth to Thy kingdom to render to Thee, His Father, all the fruits of His humanity and the glorious wounds of His Body. Let His wounds never be obscured to Thy sight, so that Thou mayest always be mindful of the atonement which Thou hast received from Him for our sins.

By virtue of this unbloody Sacrifice have mercy on me and on all sinners, as well as on all the faithful, whether they still live in the flesh or have passed from this life; and grant to us Thy grace, mercy and forgiveness of our sins, and the enjoyment of eternal life. Amen. (St. Mechtildis)

Oration

We implore Thee, omnipotent God, to grant that we, who rejoice in the Sacred Heart of Jesus and who remember the wonderful blessings we have received through His love, may also be gladdened by the fruits of these blessings.

O Lord Jesus, who didst deign to open the inexhaustible treasure of Thy Heart to Thy Church on earth, grant us the grace to live in accord with the love of this Heart and, by a most humble reverence, to repair the insults heaped upon it, who livest and reignest world without end. Amen.

Blessing

Divine Heart of my Redeemer, now that Thou hast offered Thyself in this sacrifice of the Mass for the remission of my sins and the salvation of my soul, I again bow before Thee to receive the blessing of the Triune God. May God almighty, the Father, the Son and the Holy Ghost, bless me now and forever. Amen.

End of Mass

O most sublime, most meek and most gracious Heart of my beloved Spouse, Jesus Christ, Heart of my Lord and my God, in all humility I implore Thee to guide and preserve in Thy love all the thoughts, desires and faculties of my soul, and all that I am and possess, for Thy greater honor and glory. I commend myself to Thy Heart, O merciful Jesus; I consecrate myself wholly and forever to Thee. O God, take from me my sinful and ungrateful heart, and give me a heart according to Thine own; one that will give glory to Thee forever.

O Lord, my God and Redeemer, pardon all my sins and destroy within me everything which displeases Thee; enrich my soul with every grace and virtue that pleases Thy divine Heart.

Transform me into a dwelling-place for Thy joy and Thy love. Grant that my heart may be like to Thine and my will in such agreement with Thy holy will that I may never will or desire anything except what Thou willest or desirest. May I love Thee, sweetest Jesus, my God, with my whole heart, in all and above all, now and forever. Amen. (Ven. Louis Blosius)

DEVOTION FOR CONFESSION

Before Confession

Prayer to the Holy Ghost

Come, Holy Ghost, enlighten my understanding that I may rightly know my sins; move my heart that I may truly repent of them and sincerely confess them, and strengthen my will that I may thoroughly amend my life. Amen.

Examination of Conscience

Begin your examination of conscience with a firm resolution to learn the true condition of your soul, and above all, not to seek excuses for your sins. Consider what St. John writes: "If we say that we have no sin, we deceive ourselves, and the truth is not in us. If we confess our sins, He is faithful and just to forgive us our sins and to cleanse us from all iniquity. If we say that we have not sinned, we make Him a liar, and His word is not in us" (I John 1:8-10).

If you have acquired the laudable habit of examining your conscience daily and confessing often, this present examination will be easy. Do not place too much stress on your many human imperfections. You can easily confess them to Jesus at the time of Holy Communion. Before confession recall only real faults and sins, such as deliberate distractions during prayers, neglect of the fulfillment of your duties, the sins of pride, anger, impatience, and especially the important Commandment of the love of your neighbor in thoughts, words and deeds.

If you, which God forbid, confess but seldom or have waited a long time since your last confession, then recall the Commandments of God and of the Church and take heed to remember especially the mortal sins, their number and the occasions of sins which, perhaps, you sought, or did not avoid; try to discover the kinds of sins in thought, word and deed, especially those against the first, second, third and sixth Commandments of God and the Commandments of the Church.

Contrition and Resolution

You must not postpone your contrition until a moment before confession. It is much better to excite a humble sorrow for your sins a considerable time before confession, because the spiritual return to God through contrition should urge you, like the prodigal son, to make your peace with God in the sacrament of Penance.

To stimulate real sorrow in your heart it is profitable to consider, for example, your sinful condition, the improper life you have led, the irregularities of your life and the absence of peace of conscience; or consider hell, which was created on account of sin; or heaven, the place of eternal happiness, your Father's house, which was closed to you on account of sin. Call to mind the holiness, justice, omnipotence and love of God, who created you and who has blessed you a thousandfold. Finally, picture to yourself Christ crucified, and remember that your sins have caused His sufferings. Then you say fervently:

Most beloved Father in heaven, I am profoundly sorry for my acts of disobedience and my shameful ingratitude. I detest my sins because I deserve to be severely punished for them by Thee, my Judge. Alas, through my sins I have lost Thy grace and the right to heaven. I have merited hell with all its awful tortures. But I grieve especially because by my sinfulness I have offended Thee, most gracious Father, and have been so ungrateful as to displease Thy goodness and love.

O my Saviour, during Thy life on earth Thou didst receive sinners so graciously whenever they showed signs of repentance; therefore, I firmly truth that Thou wilt not repulse my contrite heart. Thou didst shed Thy precious Blood on the cross for sinful man. Thou didst die for me also. Therefore Thou wilt not repulse me now, when, aided by thy grace, I come to Thee with the earnest intention of amending my life. I resolve never again to offend Thee; to avoid sin above all evils; to do and to suffer according to Thy holy will. Grant me the grace to serve Thee henceforth with the greatest fidelity. Amen. (Saint Alphonsus)

Prayer before Confession

O most amiable Jesus, Thou didst institute the sacrament of Penance out of love for the children of men and for the benefit of sinners, that they might be cleansed form their sins and again receive sanctifying grace. Behold, I, a poor sinner, who have sullied my soul by sin, come to Thee, with full confidence in Thy mercy, to obtain pardon in this sacrament. In order to obtain

Thy pardon I shall humbly confess to Thy representative, the priest, all the sins which I remember, no matter how hideous they may be; those sins, however, which I have forgotten, as well as all my venial sins, of which there are so many, I wish to include in this confession and acknowledge them to Thee, the true High Priest, and in presence of all the saints declare them to be disgraceful acts of disobedience against Thy holy laws and an insult to Thy Majesty. I detest all these sins from the bottom of my heart and sincerely resolve to amend my life. Grant, then, that I may hear the consoling words: "Go, in peace, thy sins are forgiven thee." I am resolved to do penance, and, in as far as I am able, to appease Thy divine justice. Amen.

Confession

The telling of one's sins should be as complete as possible, and yet short and to the point. Make no complaints about your own weakness and sinfulness. The confessor knows these things. It requires but a few words to confess what one has done or omitted to do.

After Confession

Thanksgiving

Merciful, gracious God, I give thanks to Thee now from the bottom of my heart for the inexpressible mercy which Thou hast bestowed upon me. Praised be to the infinite love of Thy Son, Jesus Christ, which has induced Him to institute this holy sacrament for the consolation of all sinners, to cleanse their souls from sin and to free them from the slavery of Satan. O my Jesus, how can I adequately thank Thee for this grace of forgiveness; how can I repay Thee for this infinite goodness and for this wonderful blessing? I was lost, and Thou didst seek and find me; I was unclean, and Thou didst wash me in Thy precious Blood and didst remove all stains of sin from me; I was sick and weary unto death, and Thou didst heal me and restore me to a new life; I was sunk in the abyss of destruction, and Thou didst raise me up to Thyself. For this inexplicable grace I render to Thee my sincerest gratitude; in union with the thanksgiving of all the holy penitents I praise and glorify Thy omnipotence, which has redeemed me; Thy infinite goodness, which did not desert me; Thy inexhaustible love, which has recreated me into a new being. (Saint Gertrude)

Prayer to the Sacred Heart

O Lord, I choose Thy Sacred Heart as my dwelling-place, that It may be my strength against temptations, the support in my weakness and my light and guide in darkness; may It supply all my wants, sanctify all my thoughts and deeds, which I desire to unite with Thine own and thus to consecrate them to Thee, so that my soul may always be prepared to receive Thee.

O Sacred Heart of Jesus, strengthen and support me in my good resolutions to love and please Thee, and grant that they may bear good fruit according to Thy divine will.

O God, be Thou my strength; do Thou aid me in all my struggles with the tempter, and preserve me from sin; I desire to be wholly and forever Thine. Amen.

"Sweet Heart of my Jesus, make me love Thee ever more and more." (Indulgence: 300 days. Plenary once a month.)

DEVOTION FOR COMMUNION

Before Holy Communion

Act of Faith

O sweetest Jesus, who will grant me the grace to behold Thy face under the white veil of the sacramental form of bread, which even the angels long to see? Who will open to me the helpful fountains of Thy five wounds, which I see with the eyes of faith on Thy Body in the Blessed Sacrament, fountains of living water to cleanse my soul from all sin? O ye fountains which flow into life eternal, pour upon me the waters of grace, which alone can quench my spiritual thirst; fill me with heavenly joy, infuse in me a faith so strong that, with Saint Thomas, the Apostle, I can say: "My Lord and my God!" Yes, I believe with unshakable faith that Thou, my Lord and my God, art truly present in the Blessed Sacrament. I would rather die a thousand times than renounce this faith. I believe that in this Sacrament Thy glorified Body is really present, more resplendent that the sun, the most perfect among millions, endowed with celestial perfection, beauty, and majesty. Here, too, is Thy Blood which was shed for the salvation of all mankind. Here, too, is Thy Soul, full of grace and wisdom, which contains all the treasures of the power and the wisdom of God. Here, finally, is Thy Divinity, namely, the almighty Word, through which the Father created all things; and because Thou art in the Father and the Father is in Thee, the heavenly Father is also present. Furthermore, the Holy Ghost is present, because of Their eternal union of love, This Sacrament is the culmination of all the miracles of Thy love. It is the greatest miracle of all and surpasses the understanding of mere creatures. This is the infallible truth, which, with Thy grace, I desire steadfastly to profess.

Act of Hope

O sweetest Jesus, I place all my hope in Thee, because Thou art my salvation and strength, my refuge and support, and because Thou art the fountain of all blessings. How could I dare to receive Thee if Thou, who gavest Thy Blood for me, didst not grant me the necessary assurance of Thy love? Trusting in Thy goodness, therefore, I approach Thee like a frightened sheep which runs to the shepherd, like an ailing man who hastens to a physician, like a condemned man who seeks a defender; Thus I come to Thee, that Thou mayest protect, heal and strengthen me. Thou hast placed the abyss of Thy love on the scales to counterbalance the abyss of my nothingness; for even if my sins, numerous as they are, were much more numerous and punishable, they would be as nothing compared to Thy mercy and the merits of Thy precious Blood. Upon this truth I place my trust, and I rejoice that there is nothing in me on which I can depend for aid. Have mercy on me and save me, O Jesus, who dost never fail those who hope in Thee. Amen.

Act of Love

How great must have been the power of Thy love, O sweetest Jesus, when, about to leave this world to go to Thy heavenly Father, Thou didst prepare a banquet for us which contains all sweetness and bliss! It was indeed an astounding act of Thy love to humble Thyself and to become man; but it is still more sublime and wonderful that Thou didst give us Thy Flesh as food and Thy Blood as drink. Thou didst bestow upon us all the treasures of Thy grace, so that we, overwhelmed by this infinite love, might manifest our love for Thee. Therefore, I love Thee as my only consolation in this vale of tears, as the only hope of my weary soul, as my only happiness and my greatest blessing on earth. I love Thee with my whole heart, with my whole soul and with all my strength. Would that I could love Thee ever more and more fervently! All my longing and sighs, all the desires of my heart, tend toward this end. Thou drawest to Thyself all the faculties of my soul while coming int my heart, making me, as far as possible, like unto Thee, feeding and satisfying my hungry soul, not with earthly food, but with Thine own most precious Flesh and Blood.

O my God, I love Thee because of this thy inexpressible generosity. Deign to inflame Thy love in me ever more and more, O Jesus, Who art the food and nourishment of love.

O Fire, which ever burns but is not consumed, enflame my whole heart that it may burn for love of Thee. Thou didst come to bring fire upon the earth; enkindle and inflame it, that it may reach into all parts of the earth. Alas, I shall never be able to love Thee as thou deservest to be loved.

Act of Desire

As the hart panteth after the fountain of water, so my soul longeth for Thee, my Savior and Lord, Jesus Christ. Yes, my soul desires to approach Thee, to offer Thee in this holy Mass to God, the Father, and joyously to draw the sweet wine from the fountain of salvation. I have become faint on the way of sin and I thirst after Thee, my God, the fountain of living waters. Hungry and thirsty I come to Thee, my Redeemer, and say: "Son of David, have mercy on me!" Give me Thy Bread, that my soul may be refreshed. Would that I had the burning desires of all the saints, that I might always long for Thee, the fountain of life, the fountain of wisdom, the fountain of eternal light, the source of all happiness. Would that my heart my ever hunger after Thee, the Bread of angels, the comfort of holy souls! Would that the innermost recesses of my soul were filled with the joy of Thy sweetness. My soul is disconsolate when not in possession of Thee, O Heart of Jesus. I long for Thee with the devotion of all the elect who eat at Thy holy table. Mayest Thou alone be my joy, my rest, my food, my treasure, and the dwelling-place of my soul.

Act of Humility

Infinite, sublime, almighty and incomprehensible God, Who art Thou, and what am I, that Thou shouldst deign to come to me, to prepare a feast for me and to take up Thy abode in me. I marvel at this Thy condescension when I think of my misery and ingratitude. Thou art the King of kings, the Lord of lords. The earth trembles in Thy presence. Thou art the source of all holiness, in whose sight the angels are not perfect. Thou art the sun of eternal brightness, enthroned in impenetrable light. I, on the contrary, am an impure creature, subject to wants of every kind, disquieted by foolish desires and humbled by my pride, a vessel of shame, a child of utter darkness. How dare I, a worm of the earth, approach Thee? Where shall I find the necessary confidence to appear before Thee, O most righteous Judge, in whose presence the pillars of heaven tremble in fear? And yet I, who am but dust and ashes, will pray to Thee. Look with mercy upon me, thy servant, Oh Lord, and receive me, whom Thou hast graciously invited to Thy holy Banquet. Behold, I am now fully aware that I am nothing and can do nothing; neither can salvation nor life be obtained without Thee. Pardon my sins, and come to me, because I, who am unworthy of Thy friendship, have returned to Thee. I sincerely trust in the words of the Prophet: "A contrite and humbled heart, O God, Thou wilt not despise" (Ps. 50:19). Amen.

After Holy Communion

O Lord, Jesus Christ, joy of my heart, I love Thee. I love Thee, my greatest and only God, with my whole heart, with my whole soul and with all my strength. Though my love be ever so imperfect, at least I earnestly desire to love Thee; and should even this desire lack in eagerness, at least I wish to have it strengthened. O Lord, enflame my heart with the fire of Thy love; and since Thou dost not ask anything but love from me, grant me the grace of this love, and I shall willingly make any sacrifice for love of Thee. If Thou dost not grant me the good will and the grace to act according to it, I shall perish miserably. O let me take heed of Thy sweet and powerful voice. If Thou wilt, Thou canst purify and enlighten me and cast elevate me to the highest pinnacle of love. Long ago Thou didst suffer and die for me; grant that now the fruits of Thy Passion and Death will become manifest in me. Remember Thy precious words, upon which I place all my trust; "He that eateth My Flesh, and drinketh My Blood, abideth in Me, and I in him" (Saint John 6:57). How sweet and heavenly are these words! Thou in me, and I in Thee! O what sublime love! Thou in me, who am the lowest creature; and I in Thee, my God, the incomprehensible majesty. One grace only is necessary, and that grace I beg of Thee: to live in Thee, to rest in Thee, never again to be separated from Thee. Happy is he who seeks Thee; happier the one who has found Thee; happiest of all is he who perseveres in Thee until death.

Thanksgiving

O infinitely good God, I thank Thee for having deigned to permit me to partake of Thy life-giving feast. I am but dust and ashes, and yet Thou didst descend from heaven and, by Thy most pure Blood, didst cleanse my soul from every stain of sin. Who am I that Thou wouldst satisfy the hunger of my weary soul, not with the manna of the desert, but with Thy immaculate Flesh? The heavens cannot contain Thee, and even the angels are not perfect in Thy sight; how is it possible then that Thou didst come to live with me? O King of infinite majesty, what didst Thou find in me that constrained Thee to leave the palace of Thy glory and to live in the abyss of my misery? All ye holy angels and saints, come and behold what great things the Lord has done to me. Although I was poor and miserable, so that I did not dare to raise my eyes to heaven, He has raised me out of the dust of the earth, made me equal to princes and kings, and has invited me to eat at His holy Table all the days of my life. Do you, my dearest friends, give thanks to Him for me, because I am still a child, not in years, indeed, but in understanding, and cannot find words with which to express my gratitude for such a wonderful grace. No matter how great my love for God may be, it does not deserve to be called love but ice and coldness. Every act of praise, adoration and homage of my poor heart melts into nothingness before His infinite perfections and dignity. O gracious and merciful God, full of goodness and love, Thou knowest my weakness and therefore wilt not disdain my humble act of thanksgiving, but wilt deign to accept my words of gratitude. Thine is the splendor and magnificence; Thine be also the honor and glory throughout all eternity. May all the races, nations and tongues of the world, all the angels and the saints, join in praising and thanking Thee; because Thy mercies are manifest in me, and Thy compassion extends over all Thy creatures. They all rejoice in Thee; may my heart also rejoice, together with my soul and all the faculties of my body. To Thee be honor and glory, for all things are of Thee, through Thee and in Thee. Thou art our God, praised and glorified forever and ever. Amen.

Petition

Most amiable Lord Jesus Christ, who hast strengthened me with Thy most pure Body and precious Blood, I earnestly implore Thee not to look upon my unworthiness, and to pardon any negligence which I may have shown in the reception of this holy Sacrament. May Thy goodness annihilate everything sinful within me. Wash me in the Tears which Thou didst shed for my sake; anoint me with the myrrh of Thy sufferings; bind me with Thy fetters, and purify me with Thy Blood. Life me up again by Thy cross, and through Thy death grant me renewed life. Implant Thy love into my heart and cast out from it all other love. Convert my whole being into Thyself, so that it may be dissolved in Thee and that I may find rest only in Thee. In order to work out my salvation Thou didst wish never to be without Thy cross; oh, grant that my heart may also have an earnest desire for crosses and humiliations.

Do not permit me to leave Thy holy banquet table without having received the fruits thereof, but grant that Thy holy Sacrament may be fruitful in me as it was in the saints. Grant that I, by the strength of this sacred food, may advance to the very pinnacle of perfection. Furthermore, O Lord, grant Thy peace, salvation and blessing to all those of Thy servants for whom I am in duty bound to pray. Convert poor sinners, call back to Thy Fold the erring and those who are separated from the unity of Thy Church; enlighten the unbelievers, who know Thee not. Give aid to all who are in need. Be gracious to all my relatives, friends and benefactors. Have mercy on my enemies. Hasten to aid all those who have recommended themselves to my prayers. Grant Thy pardon and grace to the living and the light of eternal life to the poor souls in purgatory. Amen.

INDULGENCED PRAYERS

Prayer to Jesus Crucified

Look down upon me, good and gentle Jesus, while before Thy face I humbly kneel, and with burning soul pray and beseech Thee to fix deep in my heart lively sentiments of faith, hope and charity, true contrition for my sins, and a firm purpose of amendment; while I contemplate with great love and tender pity Thy five wounds, pondering over them within me and calling to mind the words which David, the Prophet, said of Thee, my Jesus: "They have pierced My hands and My feet; they have numbered all My bones." *Our Father, Hail Mary, Glory Be once for the intentions of the Holy Father. A Plenary Indulgence, applicable to the poor souls, may be gained by those who, having confessed with sorrow and having received Holy Communion worthily, shall recite this prayer devoutly before an image or picture of Christ crucified. 10 years each time when said before an image of the Crucifix.*

Anima Christi

Soul of Christ, be my sanctification.
Body of Christ, be my salvation.
Blood of Christ, fill all my veins.
Water from the side of Christ, wash out my stains.
Passion of Christ, my comfort be.
O good Jesu, listen to me.
In Thy wounds, I fain would hide.
Ne'er to be parted from Thy side.
Guard me should the foe assail me.
Call me when my life shall fail me.
Bid me come to Thee above,
With the saints to sing Thy love,
World without end. Amen.

Indulgence: 300 days each time. Seven years if said after Communion. Plenary once a month under the usual conditions.

Prayer to Christ the King

O Christ Jesus, I acknowledge Thee as King of the universe. All that exists has been created for Thee. Make full use of Thy rights over me.

I renew the promises I made in Baptism, when I renounced Satan and all his pomps and works, and I promise to live a good Christian life. Very particularly do I pledge myself to strive, as far as I can, for the triumph of the rights of God and of Thy Church.

Divine Heart of Jesus, I offer Thee my poor efforts to obtain that all hearts may acknowledge Thy sacred Kingship, and that thus Thy reign of peace may be established in the entire world. (Plenary once a day.)

Jesus, King and center of all hearts, through the advent of Thy Kingdom, grant us peace. (Indulgence: 300 days.)

My Lord and my God. (7 years when said at the Elevation of the Holy Host, or before the Blessed Sacrament solemnly exposed. Plenary once a week.)

Blessed and praised be the Sacred Heart and the Precious Blood of Jesus in the most Holy Sacrament of the Altar. (Indulgence: 300 days.)

Eucharistic Heart of Jesus, increase in us Faith, Hope and Charity. (Indulgence: 300 days.)

Eucharistic Heart of Jesus, furnace of divine charity, give peace to the world. (Indulgence: 300 days.)

I adore Thee, O most Sacred Eucharistic Heart of Jesus. (Indulgence: 300 days.)

Praise, adoration, love and thanksgiving be every moment given to the Eucharistic Heart of Jesus in all the tabernacles of the world, and unto the end of time. Amen. (Indulgence: 300 days.)

O most Sacred Heart of Jesus, O Fount of every good, I adore Thee, I love Thee, and repent sincerely for my sins. I offer Thee this my poor heart. Do Thou make it humble, patient, pure, and in all things conformed to Thy will. Grant that I may live in Thee and for Thee. Protect me in dangers, console me in afflictions; grant me health in body, succor in temporal needs, Thy blessing upon all my works, and the grace of a happy death. (Indulgence: 500 days.)

Sweet Heart of Jesus, have mercy on us and on our erring brethren. (Indulgence: 300 days.)

Jesus, Mary, Joseph. (7 years. Plenary once a month.)

Jesus, Mary and Joseph, I give you my heart and my soul.
Jesus, Mary and Joseph, assist me in my last agony.
Jesus, Mary and Joseph, may I breathe forth my soul in peace with Thee. (7 years for each invocation each time. Plenary once a month for each invocation.)

Litany of the Most Holy Name of Jesus
Lord, have mercy on us.
Christ, have mercy on us.
Lord, have mercy on us.
Jesus, hear us.
Jesus, graciously hear us.
God the Father of heaven, * have mercy on us.
God the Son, Redeemer of the world, *
God the Holy Ghost, *
Holy Trinity, one God, *
Jesus, Son of the living God, *
Jesus, splendor of the Father, *
Jesus, brightness of eternal light, *
Jesus, King of glory, *
Jesus, the Sun of justice, *
Jesus, Son of the Virgin Mary, *
Jesus, amiable, *
Jesus, admirable, *
Jesus, the mighty God, *
Jesus, Father of the world to come, *

Jesus, Angel of the great council, *
Jesus, most powerful, *
Jesus, most patient, *
Jesus, most obedient, *
Jesus, meek and humble of Heart, *
Jesus, lover of chastity, *
Jesus, lover of us, *
Jesus, God of peace, *
Jesus, Author of life, *
Jesus, Model of all virtues, *
Jesus, zealous for souls, *
Jesus, our God, *
Jesus, our refuge, *
Jesus, Father of the poor, *
Jesus, Treasure of the faithful, *
Jesus, good Shepherd, *
Jesus, true Light, *
Jesus, eternal Wisdom, *
Jesus, infinite Goodness, *
Jesus, our Way and our Life, *
Jesus, joy of Angels, *
Jesus, King of Patriarchs, *
Jesus, Master of the Apostles, *
Jesus, Teacher of the Evangelists, *
Jesus, strength of Martyrs, *
Jesus, light of Confessors, *
Jesus, purity of Virgins, *
Jesus, crown of all Saints, *
Be merciful, spare us, O Jesus.
Be merciful, graciously hear us, O Jesus.
From all evil, * deliver us, O Jesus.
From all sin, *
From Thy wrath, *
From the snares of the devil, *
From the spirit of fornication, *
From eternal death, *
From the neglect of Thy inspirations, *
By the mystery of Thy holy Incarnation, *
By Thy Nativity, *
By Thy infancy, *

By Thy most divine life, *
By Thy labors, *
By Thy Agony and Passion, *
By Thy Cross and dereliction, *
By Thy languors, *
By Thy Death and burial, *
By Thy Resurrection, *
By Thy Ascension, *
By Thy institution of the Most holy Eucharist, *
By Thy joys, *
By Thy glory, *
Lamb of God, who takest away the sins of the world, spare us, O Jesus.
Lamb of God, who takest away the sins of the world, graciously hear us, O Jesus.
Lamb of God, who takest away the sins of the world, have mercy on us, O Jesus.
Jesus, hear us.
Jesus, graciously hear us.

Let Us Pray

O Lord Jesus Christ, who hast said: "Ask and you shall receive, seek, and you shall find, knock, and it shall be opened unto you," mercifully attend to our supplications, and grant us the gift of Thy divine charity, that we may ever love Thee with our whole heart, and never desist from Thy praise.

Give us, O Lord, a perpetual fear and love of Thy holy name; for Thou never ceasest to govern those whom Thou instructest in the solidity of Thy love. Who livest and reignest one God, world without end. Amen.

(Indulgence: 7 years. Plenary once a month with oration.)

Litany of the Blessed Virgin

Lord, have mercy on us.
Christ, have mercy on us.
Lord, have mercy on us.
Christ, hear us.
Christ, graciously hear us.
God the Father of heaven, have mercy on us.

God the Son, Redeemer of the world, have mercy on us.
God the Holy Ghost, have mercy on us.
Holy Trinity, One God, have mercy on us.
Holy Mary, * pray for us.
Holy Mother of God, *
Holy Virgin of virgins, *
Mother of Christ, *
Mother of divine grace, *
Mother most pure, *
Mother most chaste, *
Mother inviolate, *
Mother undefiled, *
Mother most amiable, *
Mother most admirable, *
Mother of good counsel, *
Mother of our Creator, *
Mother of our Saviour, *
Virgin most prudent, *
Virgin most venerable, *
Virgin most renowned, *
Virgin most powerful, *
Virgin most merciful, *
Virgin most faithful, *
Mirror of justice, *
Seat of wisdom, *
Cause of our joy, *
Spiritual vessel, *
Vessel of honor, *
Singular vessel of devotion, *
Mystical rose, *
Tower of David, *
Tower of ivory, *
House of gold, *
Ark of the covenant, *
Gate of heaven, *
Morning star, *
Health of the sick, *
Refuge of sinners, *
Comforter of the afflicted, *
Help of Christians, *

Queen of Angels, *
Queen of Patriarchs, *
Queen of Prophets, *
Queen of Apostles, *
Queen of Martyrs, *
Queen of Confessors, *
Queen of Virgins, *
Queen of all Saints, *
Queen conceived without original sin, *
Queen assumed into Heaven, *
Queen of the most holy Rosary, *
Queen of peace, *
Lamb of God, who takest away the sins of the world, spare us, O Lord.
Lamb of God, who takest away the sins of the world, graciously hear us, O Lord.
Lamb of God, who takest away the sins of the world, have mercy on us.
V. Pray for us, O holy Mother of God,
R. That we may be made worthy of the promises of Christ.
Indulgence: 7 years. Plenary once a month. The Oration must be added to gain the indulgence.

Let Us Pray

Pour forth, we beseech Thee, O Lord, Thy grace into our hearts; that we, to whom the Incarnation of Christ, Thy Son, was made known by the message of an angel, may by His Passion and Cross, be brought to the glory of His Resurrection; through the same Christ, our Lord. Amen.

May the divine assistance remain always with us. May the souls of the faithful departed, through the mercy of God, rest in peace. Amen.

"We fly to thy patronage, O holy Mother of God, despise not our petitions in our necessities; but deliver us from all dangers, O ever glorious and blessed Virgin. Amen."

(Indulgence: 5 years. Plenary once a month, also at the hour of death, for those who have said this prayer during their life.)

Litany in Honor of St. Joseph

Lord, have mercy on us.
Christ, have mercy on us.
Lord, have mercy on us.
Christ, hear us.
Christ, graciously hear us.
God the Father of Heaven, have mercy on us.
God the Son, Redeemer of the world, have mercy on us.
God the Holy Ghost, have mercy on us.
Holy Trinity, one God, have mercy on us.
Holy Mary, pray for us.
St. Joseph, pray for us.
Illustrious scion of David, pray for us.
Light of patriarchs, pray for us.
Spouse of the Mother of God, pray for us.
Chaste guardian of the Virgin, pray for us.
Foster-father of the Son of God, pray for us.
Diligent defender of Christ, pray for us.
Head of the Holy Family, pray for us.
Joseph most just, pray for us.
Joseph most chaste, pray for us.
Joseph most prudent, pray for us.
Joseph most valiant, pray for us.
Joseph most obedient, pray for us.
Joseph most faithful, pray for us.
Mirror of patience, pray for us.
Lover of poverty, pray for us.
Model of workers, pray for us.
Ornament of domestic life, pray for us.
Guardian of virgins, pray for us.
Safeguard of families, pray for us.
Consolation of the poor, pray for us.
Hope of the sick, pray for us.
Patron of the dying, pray for us.
Terror of demons, pray for us.
Protector of the holy Church, pray for us.
Lamb of God, who takest away the sins of the world, spare us, O Lord.
Lamb of God, who takest away the sins of the world, graciously hear us, O Lord.

Lamb of God, who takest away the sins of the world, have mercy on us.
V. He has made him master of His house,
R. And prince over all His possessions.

Let us pray.

O God, who in Thy ineffable providence didst vouchsafe to choose blessed Joseph to be the spouse of Thy most holy Mother, grant we beseech Thee, that we may be worthy to have him for our intercessor in heaven, who livest and reignest, world without end. Amen. *(Indulgence: 5 years. Plenary once a month.)*